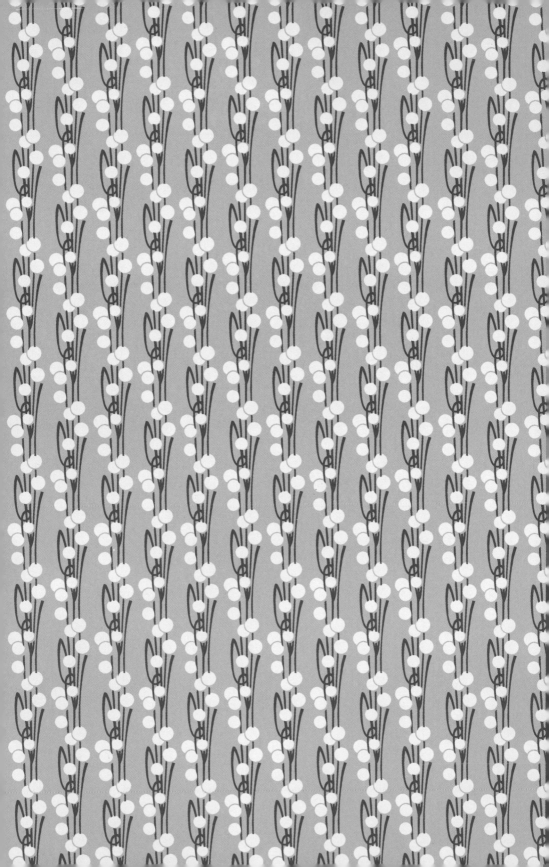

75 Exciting Vegetables for Your Garden

75 Exciting Vegetables
for Your Garden

Jack Staub

ILLUSTRATIONS BY
Ellen Sheppard Buchert

Gibbs Smith, Publisher
Salt Lake City

First Edition

09 08 07 06 05   5 4 3 2 1

PUBLISHED BY
Gibbs Smith, Publisher
PO Box 667
Layton, Utah 84041

ORDERS: 1.800.748.5439
www.gibbs-smith.com

DESIGNED BY Kurt Wahlner and Steve Rachwal

Library of Congress Cataloging-in-Publication Data

Staub, Jack
75 exciting vegetables for your garden / Jack Staub ; illustrations by
Ellen Buchert.— 1st ed.
p. cm.
ISBN 1-58685-250-7
1. Vegetable gardening. 2. Vegetables. 3. Vegetables — Pictorial works.
I. Title: Seventy-five exciting vegetables for your garden. II. Title.

SB321.S665 2005
635–dc22   2004021516

Dedication

This book is dedicated to
Renny Reynolds, Bob and Rose Ritchie,
my godfather Peter G. Renehan,
and my parents Jack and Faith Hussey Staub,
without any and all of whom
I would be more impossible than I am to date

❦ Contents ❦

⚜ Introduction ⚜

I concede immediately that, while I have attempted to make this volume unique in content and tone, I have, in truth, had a singularly superb model for it. In fact, I have been sorely tempted to entitle this work *Eminent Vegetables,* so highly do I esteem Lytton Strachy's brilliant *Eminent Victorians,* that early twentieth-century paragon of biographical brevity and wit. In it, Mr. Strachy serves up four brief, laserlike portraits of the Victorian luminaries Florence Nightingale, Cardinal Newman, General Gordon, and Dr. Manning. Each profile is as notable for its succinct and wry appraising tone as it is for its erudition, psychological insight, and historical elucidation. In a single stroke, Strachy managed to blow the academic dust off the art of biography, noting rather accurately that "...it is perhaps as difficult to write a good life as to live one."

In this volume my intention is to present you, the reader, with portraits not of famous personalities of our time, but of vegetables whose time I feel has come. Eminent vegetables. Entrancing vegetables. Heirloom and hybrid. Native and transplant. Seventy-five really superb vegetables in current culture that are as exciting for their physical beauty as they are for their taste. Today, the entire world is our horticultural oyster and, originating in every corner of the globe, each of these vegetables is possessed of both a savor and an aesthetic charm that would make the loveliest blossom hang its head. As well, each is entirely suited to American cultivation, yet most of these varieties are perhaps totally unknown to the laissez-faire gardener. In short, I feel that these are vegetables with which every serious American vegetable gardener should be acquainted.

That said, I have defiantly stretched the boundaries of both cultivation and cultivar in this volume to include some vegetable varieties that will definitely need to be started indoors in most of our American climates, and others that are not really vegetables at all, but fruits (tomatoes, eggplants) or berries (melons). Ultimately, I suppose, my definitions on both of these fronts have grown to include anything I happen to grow in my own kitchen garden. Certainly, like *Webster's* and the United States Supreme Court, we can broaden the definition of the word *vegetable* to include any plant "grown for an edible part...usually eaten with the principle part of a meal." Melons, I agree, are rather a stretch, but there you have it.

You will also note that in introducing these wonderful vegetables in alphabetical order, I have chosen, rather willy-nilly, to list some by species and others by variety. This had as much to do with the resultant "mix" of plants and information as it did with botanical accuracy. Anyway, my call entirely and you are perfectly at liberty to disagree. It is also my intention in this book to present you with a new look at what is certainly an old-fashioned format, much as Mr. Strachy did with the art of biography. I have purposefully steered away from glossy photographs and a larger scale design to give you a small, illustrated book that hopefully has the charm, decorativeness, and durability of those wonderful, informative books of the past, which sought to enlighten and amuse as they instructed.

Therefore, in each of these plant portraits, I have endeavored to be brief but thorough, horticulturally sound yet light of touch, offering up a dose of surprising history, a scrap of unexpected lore, or a tidbit of culinary insight in a manner that, with any luck, lifts these profiles above the usual, stolid meat-and-potatoes of cultivation, soil preference, and so on, to a level of fundamental literary enjoyment. As Lytton Strachy so accurately opined: "To preserve a becoming brevity, which excludes everything that is redundant and nothing that is significant: that, surely, is the first duty of the biographer. The second, no less surely, is to maintain his own freedom of spirit."

In all these things, I heartily hope that I have succeeded to the reader's satisfaction.

AMARANTH 'JOSEPH'S COAT'

❧ 1. Amaranth 'Joseph's Coat' ❧
Amaranthus tricolor

Following their introduction into Europe, amaranths were thought to be of such sacred significance that, in 1693, Queen Christina of Sweden founded the mystical "Order of the Amaranth," which survives to this day as the highest order of the Eastern Star Chapter of North American Masons, America's largest Masonic women's organization.

Amaranths are ancient tropical plants of diverse and surprising beauty, and are believed to have originated in India, although they have been grown throughout Mexico and South America since at least the third millennium B.C. A relative of common Lamb's Quarters as well as the Garden Cockscomb, there are about sixty species of amaranth, grown either for their tassel-like seed heads, which are ground as a grain, or for their edible leaves, which are used as a potherb. Amaranths found their way into Greece very early on as well, the Greeks believing them to be immortal, and both this fascinating plant's botanical and common names find their root in the Greek *amarantos,* meaning "never-fading." We also know that Artemis of Esephus, the many-breasted Greek earth goddess, regarded them as sacred.

The Aztec emperor Montezuma held the amaranth in such high regard that he demanded 200,000 bushels of seed a year of it in tribute from his subjects, and in the Aztec culture, the amaranth was mystically associated with human sacrifice. This practice apparently appalled the conquistadores, who were fairly appalling themselves if stones are to be thrown and, consequently, further cultivation of amaranth in the former Aztec nation was forbidden, causing amaranth as a food crop to fall into obscurity on the American continent for hundreds of years. On other continents, however, amaranth continued to be a vegetable of great importance, particularly in the tropics of Africa and Asia, and today is under extensive cultivation in China, India, Africa, and Europe, as well as in North and South America.

In 1786, when he was ambassador to France, Thomas Jefferson included the 'Joseph's Coat' variety of amaranth in a shipment of interesting seeds to his brother-in-law Francis Eppes, in Virginia. A variety grown for its edible leaves, Joseph's Coat is perhaps the most striking of amaranths and will certainly deliver a spectacular jolt of color to any vegetable garden. Its name, of course, derives from the Genesis 37 tale of Joseph's "coat of many colors," which his brothers stained red with blood in order to make his father believe he was dead. As gaudy as a coleus, with which it is often confused, Joseph's Coat boasts almost supernaturally brilliant cadmium yellow and carmine foliage on plants growing to 4 feet, the whole carnival of it topped with scarlet-plumed seed heads. This, in fact, is a plant so brazenly decorative, one is tempted to consider it far too exotically beautiful to be edible.

Being a true tropical trooper, Joseph's Coat not only likes things hot but is incredibly heat, drought, and soil tolerant as well when planted in a warm, well-lit spot. Therefore, direct sow Joseph's Coat seeds after last frost in a sunny (and visually prominent) place in your garden, thinning to 3 feet apart. The leaves, rich in vitamins A and C, calcium and iron, and tasting much like spinach, can be employed culinarily in much the same way as spinach, although, like many living things, they are best eaten when young. Additionally, because they will fade when cooked, why not try the tiniest leaves in a summer salad mix, where they will add an eye-catching note of color. Leave the rest to startle the eye in the garden.

ॐ

❧ 2. Artichoke 'Violetto di Romagna' ❧
Cynara scolymus

In Scotland in the nineteenth century, artichokes were so highly valued
that it was thought only prosperous men should have the right to grow
them and that it would be impertinent for a lesser man to even attempt
such a folly.

The artichoke is actually the edible flower bud of a large, thistle-like plant of the sunflower family that is native to the Mediterranean and Near East, its common name coming to us from the Arabic *al kharshuf.* The Moroccan invaders brought the artichoke to Spain in the ninth or tenth century, whence it became *alcahofa,* the Italians subsequently turning it to *carciofa.* The Romans were fond of having artichokes imported from Carthage and Cordova for their banquets, and thought the plants' spines looked like the teeth of Cynara, the dog of mythological tales, thus this cultivar's Latin sobriquet *Cynara scolymus.*

In the first century A.D., the Roman naturalist Pliny noted, though not with great pleasure, that in his time the artichoke was held in higher esteem than any other potherb in Rome, further commenting that even donkeys were smart enough to refuse to eat them. Introduced into England in 1548, an amusing piece of Elizabethan folklore held that the artichoke was created when an ill-tempered beauty angered the gods and was transformed by them into a prickly thistle, a form more suitable to her personality. At the turn of the nineteenth century, the German poet Goethe was, like Pliny, apparently appalled by the continental taste for artichokes, exclaiming incredulously in his *Travels Through Italy:* "The peasants eat thistles!"

Like many antique vegetables, artichokes were prescribed by ancient physicians for all kinds of physical ailments, from jaundice and coughs to the faltering libidos of men, the French herbalists Estienne and Liebault coyly suggesting in the sixteenth century that a diet rich in

ARTICHOKE 'VIOLETTO DI ROMAGNA'

artichoke extracts could cure "weakness of the generative parts." The juice, when pressed from the plant before it blossomed, was also used as a wildly popular hair restorative. Currently, the world's main growers of artichokes are Italy, Spain, Argentina, Morocco, and the United States, where the Swiss who first established the vineyards in California's Salinas Valley also founded the booming Pajaro Valley artichoke industry, now a $50 million a year crop.

The Italians have made selections of both purple and green artichokes since the fifteenth century, the purple varieties, historically, thought to be more tender than green types. The regal and prettily named 'Violetto di Romagna' is an ancient Italian heirloom: a large, round-headed, imperial beauty possessed of buds dramatically blushed with a deep royal purple, surrounded by the requisite, exquisite froth of deeply serrated, silvery leaves. If I had to pick one major piece of architecture to anchor a vegetable bed or add visual punch to a mixed border, 'Violetto di Romagna' would be it.

Artichokes thrive in the cool, wet, temperate, coastal climes of central California, where they grow to a truly stately 5 feet tall. When grown as perennials, they have a life span of about five years and are propagated in winter or spring from root divisions. Divisions should be spaced 4 to 6 feet apart, with the growth buds or shoots just above the soil surface. These recipe tips from John Evelyn's *Acetaria* of 1699, when applied to the infant buds, are as delicious now as they were back then: "The heads being split in quarters first eaten raw with oyl, a little vinegar, salt and pepper . . . they are likewise, while tender and small, fried in fresh butter crisp with persley."

3. Asparagus Bean
❧ (Yard Long White Snake) ❧
Vigna unguinculata sesquipedalis

Pythagoras, the great Greek mathematician and author of that famous theorem repugnant to all right-brained individuals, held the decidedly unscientific and, furthermore, highly unlikely belief that human souls transmigrated into beans after death.

Man, it seems, has always had somewhat of a love-hate relationship with the bean. In ancient Rome, for instance, a pontifex of the official Roman religion was forbidden to eat or even utter the word *bean* as funerals generally ended with a feast of beans and they were, therefore, considered inauspicious. In Egypt, priests considered them unclean. Whether this was at all related to the Pythagorian theory that that darling fava on your plate might by harboring the soul of your dear departed mama is unknown.

This is the story of a bean that has extremely little in common with asparagus save that it is thought by some to have a slightly "asparagusy" flavor. Far better the common name given it in the Orient, Yard Long White Snake, which, if somewhat overdramatically, at least gives one a fairly accurate visual picture, for this is a bean unlike any bean you have ever seen. Also known as the Yardlong Bean, Long Horn Bean, and Chinese Longbean, it is a vigorous climber that produces the palest of celadon green pods (there are also darker green and purple varieties) with the faintest rosy tip.

However, what is most remarkable about these beans, aside from the fact that they grow in pretty, matching pairs like Siamese twins, is that they range from an astounding 14 to 30 inches long. If not yard long (the sesquipedalis in the botanical name means " foot and a half"), they are at least *very* long. And, as if this were not adequate visual majesty, consider also their pretty yellow to violet blue flowers borne on strong, trailing vines, often reaching heights of 9 to 12 feet.

A cousin to the cowpea or black-eyed pea, the Asparagus Bean is a subtropical/tropical plant widely grown in southeastern Asia, Thailand and southern China and, when purchasable elsewhere, is usually only found in Asian markets. However, it is interesting to note that beans came to China only in about A.D. 1200 along the silk routes. Therefore, the origin of the Asparagus Bean is somewhat obscure, for beans have been found in the remnants of virtually every known early civilization, from Bronze Age settlements in Switzerland to the Aztec ruins of Peru.

At any rate, being another tropical sort, the Asparagus Bean is sensitive to temperature and will be fairly miserable if planted out when it's too cold and rainy in spring. As well, like many tropicals, they're fairly long season plants (80 to 90 days). Therefore, start them indoors in 4-inch pots 4 to 6 weeks before your frost date, providing a stake in each pot for the plants to vine around. Transplant out only when soil and nighttime temperatures are above the 60-degree mark, providing some strong trellising or a good-sized teepee. By August, you should be harvesting a substantial and delicious crop. The startling pods are crisp, tender and possessed of a slightly nutty (some think "asparagusy") flavor. To prepare, I like to cut them into manageable segments, steam until just tender, then toss in a hot pan with a clove of garlic, a drizzle of walnut oil and some toasted, chopped walnuts. Heaven.

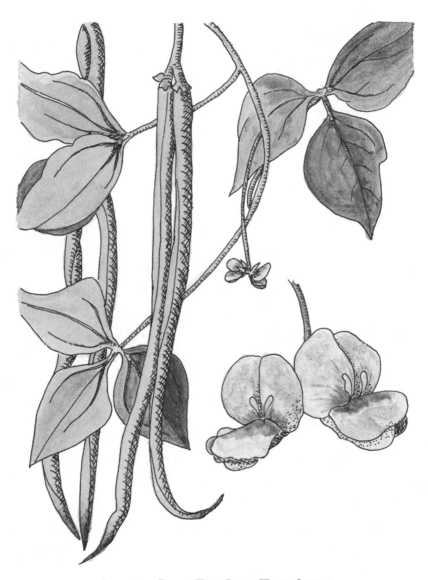

ASPARAGUS BEAN (YARD LONG WHITE SNAKE)

❧ 4. Asparagus Pea ❧
Tetragonobolus pupureus

"These Pease, which by their great increase did such good to the poore
. . . without doubt grew there many years before, but were not
observed till hunger made them take notice of them, and quickened their
invention, which commonly in our people is very dull, especially in
finding out food of this nature."

—John Gerard, *The Herball*, 1636

The pea is another of those vegetables known to virtually all of our earliest civilizations. In fact, one can actually trace the expansion of Stone Age farming by its carbonized remains as it traveled from Nea Nikmedia in Greece in 5500 B.C. to the Nile Delta in 5000 B.C., the western Mediterranean and India in 2000 B.C., and China somewhere between 916 and 618 B.C. A pot was discovered on the site of Homeric Troy containing 440 pounds of peas, and Theophrastus, friend of Aristotle and pupil of Plato, mentions peas in his fourth century *History of Plants*. In short, an old and reliable friend.

It was the Romans who most probably introduced the cultivated pea to Britain, although it wasn't until the sixteenth century that a distinction was finally drawn between the "field" pea, which was dried then boiled later into "pease porridge," and the "garden" pea, which was eaten "green." The Asparagus Pea, though a member of the *Fabeacea* or pea family, is actually neither an asparagus nor a pea plant. Also known as the Winged Pea, Goa Bean, Princess Pea, Four-Angled Bean, and Asparagus Bean, the Asparagus Pea should not be confused with the Chinese Long Bean (*Vigna unguinculata sesquipedalis*), also known as the Asparagus Bean, to which it is totally unrelated.

An ancient tropical food plant, the Asparagus Pea most likely originated in northwest Africa, and it is still most widely grown in tropical

Asia and New Guinea. It had found its way into England by 1596, where John Gerard grew it, knowing it as "square crimson-velvet pease" although he cultivated it not as an esculent, but as a purely decorative plant, and with excellent reason. The Asparagus Pea is a truly distinctive plant with a particularly decorative, low, bushy, growing habit; unusual brick-red flowers; and the most uniquely fanciful "winged" tetragonal pods. In fact, the Asparagus Pea is so notably ornamental, it would make a very attractive potted plant if placed in a well-lit position.

Because the plant is a tropical native, I will state immediately that it takes a long (90 plus days), hot growing season for the Asparagus Pea to really get going, so if you live in the North, you'll have to start them in the greenhouse or just hope for the best. Therefore sow this remarkable vegetable specimen in the greenhouse in 3-inch pots 6 to 8 weeks before your frost date.

Germination usually takes about 7 to 14 days. Harden off and plant out 12 inches apart when soil is warmed up to above 65 degrees. If your season is long enough and you're planting outdoors, sow 4 inches apart in rows 12 inches apart. A little twiggy support will help but is not essential. Harvest the fruit when small (less than 1 inch). The best time to pick the fruit is after sunset when the leaves close up, allowing one to see those wonderful-looking pods, and I recommend cooking them whole, simply steamed with a knob of butter and a pinch of salt and pepper, allowing their delicate "asparagusy" taste to be the star. The young green leaves and shoots may also be eaten as a vegetable, and the roots used, fresh or cooked, in the manner of a Jerusalem artichoke or potato, though honestly, it takes a very long season to produce a tuber of any size. Still, for those fantastic pods and pretty flowers, give this one a try.

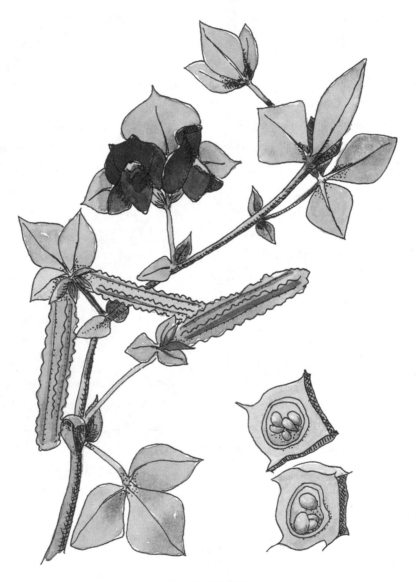

Asparagus Pea

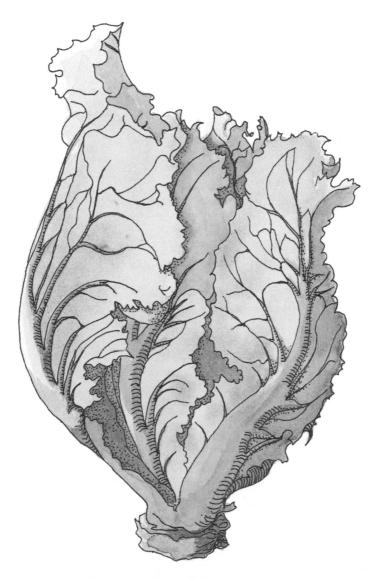

AUSTRALIAN YELLOWLEAF LETTUCE

5. Australian
❧ Yellowleaf Lettuce ❧
Lactuca sativa

In Greece, lettuce is still viewed as an "antiaphrodisiac" as, according to ancient Greek myth, the perhaps libidinally overambitious Adonis was transformed into a wilting head of lettuce by Zeus for attempting to woo Hera from him.

Lettuce is another ancient vegetable family that, while permuting into a thousand variations on a theme, has at the same time remained extremely close to its wild roots. A relative of chicory, the *Lactuca sativa* family is a descendant of the bitter wild lettuce (*Lactuca scariola*) native to Asia Minor and the trans-Caucasus. The milder, more refined var. *sativa* is believed to have originated in the Mediterranean region, but has been found growing as far afield as Europe, Africa, and the Near East since recorded time. Both the common and Latin names of lettuce have their roots in one of its most prominent characteristics: the milky, mildly soporific juice it releases when cut or bruised. The word *lettuce* derives from the French *laitue,* meaning "milky," and this genus's Latin name *Lactuca* comes from the Latin word for milk.

According to Herodotus, the virtues of lettuce, or *kahn,* were being extolled by the kings of Persia as early as the sixth century B.C., Persia also being home to one of the more prominently unfortunate pieces of vegetable lore. It seems that, in order to avoid contention over the throne in the earliest days of his reign, the Emperor Cambyses had his younger brother Smerdis put to death. One day soon afterwards, his grief-stricken sister plucked a head of lettuce from her luncheon plate and, flamboyantly stripping away its leaves, asked her brother whether the result pleased him. When Cambyses replied that the lettuce was nothing without its leaves, his sister responded: "It is the same with our family; you have just cut off a precious sprout." Not taking this as well as he might have, Cambyses, within a matter of hours, had her put to death as well.

Many botanists feel that the loose-leaf varieties of lettuce were the earliest incarnations of the *Lactuca sativa* clan, and they have existed in a whole range of colors, stripings, and dapplings since very early in the recorded history of vegetables. However, the beautiful variety Australian Yellowleaf is pretty much unique in this vast family. True, among the varied greens and reds and bronzes of the lettuce family there are some nice, bright, yellow-green forms but, to my knowledge, there's not a single other vegetable of any breed to compare with the true, brilliant chartreuse of this enchanting Australian heirloom. Extremely large, loose-growing, frilly-edged heads are genuinely like spots of neon yellow color in the garden, providing stunning and unique contrast to the surrounding hues of its neighbors. Australian Yellowleaf Lettuce boasts the additional commendable qualities of a sweet, tender, nonfibrous texture and a winningly slow-bolting habit.

As John Gerard noted in his *Herball* of 1636, "Lettuce is a cold and moist pot-herbe . . . " and is best grown either early or late in the season, although Australian Yellowleaf will weather the heat of summer better than most. Start this sunny beauty 3 or 4 weeks before your frost date in seed cups indoors and plant out (or direct seed) after danger of frost. Thin to 8 to 10 inches apart and you should be enjoying these dazzling, frilly heads in about 50 days. Why not toss the leaves of this garden stunner with some currant tomatoes, a squeeze of lemon, a clove of garlic, a drizzle of good olive oil, and a shake each of salt and pepper?

❧ 6. Broccoli 'Romanesco' ❧
Brassica oleracea botrytis

Drusius, son of the Roman Emperor Tiberius, craved broccoli prepared in the then-popular "Apician" way to such an alarming degree that for an entire month he ate nothing else, causing his urine to turn a brilliant green and his father to take him to brutal task for his "precarious living."

Although it is usually assumed that broccoli is Italian by birth and it is, in fact, an ancient Etruscan cultivar, broccoli were actually first brought into culture by the Rasenna, who came to Italy from what is now Turkey in the eighth century B.C. They settled in what we now know as Tuscany, the broccoli they cultivated reaching Rome sometime before the fifth century A.D., when Roman farmers glowingly referred to it as "the five green fingers of Jupiter." It was also these early Romans who first referred to the Rasenna as "Tusci" or "Etrusci" and to ancient Tuscany as "Etruria." The ancient Rasenna proved to be active traders with the Greeks, Sicilians, Corsicans, and Sardinians, and so broccoli spread rapidly throughout the Greco-Roman empire.

The Tuscan-born Catherine de Medici is believed to have introduced broccoli into France, along with the artichoke and other vegetables, upon her marriage to Henry II in 1533, but the first mention of broccoli in France doesn't occur until 1560. In 1699, the English herbalist John Evelyn reported in his *Acetaria* that "the broccoli from Naples, perhaps the Halmerida of Pliny (or Athenoeus rather) . . . are very delicate . . . commended for being not so rank, but agreeable to most palates and of better nourishment." In 1724, Miller's *Gardener's Dictionary* gave another early account of broccoli, referring to it as "a stranger" in England and as "sprout colli-flower" or "Italian asparagus."

Broccoli, as a member of the *Brassica* family, is in fact closely related to cauliflower, cabbage, and Brussels sprouts, so closely in both form and genetic disposition that botanists have always had difficulty with their

BROCCOLI 'ROMANESCO'

classification. To confuse matters further, historically, broccoli, cabbage, and cauliflower were all referred to as the catchall "colewort" so, throughout their ancient travels in Europe and subsequently the New World, the three were often confused. All *Brassicas* share a common feature in that their four-petaled flowers bear a resemblance to a Greek cross, which is why they are frequently referred to as "crucifers." The name "broccoli" comes from the Latin *bracchium,* meaning "strong arm" or "branch," broccoli having many strong "branches" or "arms" growing from the stout main stem.

Broccoli 'Romanesco' is an ancient and especially beautiful variety with architectural-almost-to-the-point-of-other-worldly, spiraling, apple-green whorls composing its truly remarkable head. Due to this densely budded, nearly cauliflowerlike aspect, many botanists place this variety in that ill-defined *Brassica* shadowland of the "broccoliflower," a place somewhere between broccoli and cauliflower. However, in all opinions, the beauteous Broccoli 'Romanesco,' like all broccolis, is a jewel of nutrition, being uncommonly rich in vitamin A, potassium, folacin, iron, fiber, beta-carotene, and a host of anticarcinogens, and is thought to possess better flavor and texture than more common broccoli types.

A notable success in northern climes, Broccoli 'Romanesco' should be started indoors 4 weeks before your frost date, then plant out after danger of frost 15 inches apart in fertile soil. Expect to start harvesting 75 to 100 days from transplant. In terms of cooking, why not try it in the ancient Apician style so dear to young Drusius: steam or boil till tender, then "bruise with a mixture of cumin and coriander seeds, chopped onion, plus a few drops of oil and sun-made wine." Try not to overindulge.

❦ 7. Brussels Sprout 'Rubine' ❦
Brassica oleracea gemmifera

"The Cymae or sprouts rather of the Cole are very delicate, so boil'd as to retain their verdure and green colour. The best comes from Denmark and Russia . . . "

— John Evelyn,
Acetaria: A Discourse of Sallets, 1699

Brussels sprouts are one of those vegetables that have evolved in a swirl of controversy and conjecture. Many believe them to be an ancient European crop, descendent from the wild cabbages or coleworts of prehistory, and introduced into Belgium by Julius Caesar. Certainly, the Romans were fond of a small, edible sprout they called *Bullata gemmifera,* or "diamond-maker," due to its purported ability to make you brighter. As well, *spruyten* were included in market regulations in Belgium and *spruyts* mentioned in English markets as early as A.D. 1213. There are also numerous sixteenth-century references to an edible plant known as *sproqs,* and John Evelyn's seventeenth-century *Acetaria* reference to "sprouts," although again whether these allusions can be pinned to the things we now know as Brussels sprouts remains in doubt.

Many contemporary botanists feel that the Brussels sprout is a mid- to late-eighteenth-century invention, and was perhaps a refinement of the small-headed Milan cabbage, cultivated by the farmers of the Low Countries, and appearing on the vegetative scene after 1750. From this region it is believed by this faction that they then spread to France and England in the early nineteenth century, and finally to America and Thomas Jefferson's kitchen garden at Monticello in 1812. However, there are those who dispute even this cultivar's Flemish origin, holding that the common name derives from the nineteenth century forms most available in Europe, which happened to originate with growers near

Brussels. I hope all this information is sufficient to making the historical roots of this handsome vegetable perfectly clear.

Basically, Brussels sprouts, as members of the *Brassica* family, are tiny cabbages that grow along a stout, upright stalk, most varieties being green and all to be commended for their healthy doses of vitamin C, beta-carotene, and cancer-inhibiting agents. The Brussels Sprout 'Rubine,' however, is an heirloom variety possessed of a singular, ravishingly uniform, deep purple-red hue, stalk, leaves, and sprouts all being crimson-tinged. This unique coloration coupled with its becomingly tall architectural form makes it a particularly striking and welcome addition to any vegetable garden. As well, the few red varieties of Brussels sprout (there's a brand-new hybrid called "Falstaff" being offered this year) are thought by many to be tastier than the green types.

'Rubine' does take a longer season than most of the green ones to fruit but, that said, about 100 days from planting, you'll be rewarded by a profusion of walnut-sized buds with a deep purple coloration and a wonderful, rich, old-time flavor. Brussels sprouts are easy to grow successfully in average soil, late June or early July being the perfect time to plant for late fall harvest. Ultimately, each plant will need a 2-foot-square area in which to grow and do keep in mind that sprouts that have been exposed to one or more solid freezes are infinitely sweeter than not, so this is definitely a *late* fall crop. To harvest, begin picking at the bottom, breaking off the leaf below the sprout, then removing the sprout, as the upper sprouts will continue to mature as the lower ones are harvested. Serve these little beauties simply by incising an "x" in the base of each, lightly steaming (don't overcook!), then tossing with pine nuts and some fried, slivered pancetta and its renderings.

BRUSSELS SPROUT 'RUBINE'

❧ 8. Bull's Blood Beet ❧
Beta vulgaris

In an apparently violent flight of horticultural fancy, Thomas Hill, a sixteenth-century English herbalist, recommended watering white beets with the dregs of a good red wine to turn them into the more desirable crimson variety.

Beets are believed by some to have been cultivated in all the lands between the Caspian and Mediterranean seas and even as far away as India since the third or fourth century B.C. Beets were grown for both their tasty tops and hearty roots, though the clearly devoted leaf-eater Pliny believed the "crimson nether parts" of the beet were valuable only for their medicinal properties. Grated, boiled beet was, in fact, used by the Saxons as an ingredient in bone-salve and as an emetic, and the juice of the pounded root was recommended for all kinds of festering wounds and infectious bites, of which there were plenty in that antic time.

The fleshy 'Roman Beet' (the Italian *Bassano*), which later took Europe by storm, was first refined in the sixteenth century, followed in the eighteenth century by those two other popular early cultivars 'Flat Egyptian,' not surprisingly an Egyptian native, and the 'Long Red,' a fresh-faced English variety. Over time, selection of beet types with round (versus long, tapered) roots has changed the personality of this cultivar substantially, although modern table beets still range from flat to elongated and from red to yellow and black. Our current main beet producers are Russia, France, the United States, Poland, and Italy; in recent years American farmers have grown beets on over 14,000 acres. Healthwise, red beets in particular are believed to stimulate the immune system and have possible anticancerous properties.

The gorgeous Bull's Blood Beet is an old cultivar originally bred from the older French variety Crapaudine and known for its sweet,

BULL'S BLOOD BEET

stunningly beautiful, dark red-purple tops and remarkable flavor. It was later further refined by seedsman Kees Sahin in the Netherlands, who selected it for the darkest, most dramatically colored leaves possible. Foliage is key in a decorative potager and there is nothing more dramatic in the garden than the deep, royal crimson of these gorgeous plants and, in fact, they have been planted in purely decorative flower borders for years for the sheer spectacle of their leaves. Juice from the Bull's Blood beetroot is currently used to make the only red food coloring allowed by Swedish law, following in a long tradition of use as a temporary dye, as ladies of fashion of the nineteenth century employed beet juice to add a becoming touch of carmine to their cheeks and lips.

Beets are cool-season plants that grow best at temperatures between 60 and 65 degrees, the optimum soil temperature for seed germination being 55 to 75 degrees. Like carrots, they prefer loamy, sandy soil, as a hard clay will prevent root enlargement. Plant seeds 2 inches apart in rows 10 to 30 inches apart and ½ inch deep. Cool temperatures will result in the best red color. You can expect to start harvesting in 50 to 70 days, although optimum harvest size is 1½ to 2 inches in diameter (any larger and you run the risk of woodiness). Use this spectacular cultivar for a summery beetroot soup (steam the colorful tops for a separate treat!): boil with chopped leeks, tomatoes, and ginger, add a handful of white rice, purée with a couple of cups of cranberry juice and a dash of salt, force through a strainer (to remove skin and seeds), chill, then serve with a dollop of jalapeño- and chive-scented sour cream — a lovely study in contrasts.

❧ 9. Cabbage 'Ruby Perfection' ❧
Brassica oleracea capitata

In Greek mythology it was believed that cabbages were created when Zeus, while consulting several oracles about matters of celestial importance, was so confounded by their contradictory advice that he broke into a nervous sweat, and wherever a drop of divine perspiration hit the earth, a cabbage sprouted.

The family of *Brassicas,* or "coleworts" as they were known through much of early European history, is as wildly diverse and incestuous a group of vegetables as you will run across, with countless varieties and a whole host of disguises: among them cabbage, broccoli, cauliflower, broccoliflower, kale, Brussels sprout, cress, and mustard. Many believe that the oldest crucifers were wild mustards and that the cabbage was most probably a later generation of this far-flung dynasty, refined over many centuries to achieve its signature tight, dense ball of edible leaves. The *oleracea* was affixed to the "armed" *Brassica* due to the distinctively controversial smell of this genus, *oler* meaning "smell" in Latin, and *capitata* was added for the cabbage's "head"-ing growth habit.

Cabbages are thought to be Mediterranean in origin, the earliest *Brassica oleracea capitata,* or heart or apple cabbage, being introduced by the Emperor Claudius and his invading Romans into Britain around A.D. 43. In Rome, cabbage was highly regarded as a cure for melancholy, and was applied as a poultice for sores and tumors as well, and in his *De Re Rustica,* Cato commended it, raw and pickled, for its effectiveness in counteracting the effects of alcohol. In fact, the Greeks, Romans, and Egyptians, in general, believed that wine and cabbage were natural opponents in the battle for sobriety and that the latter, being a heartier, brawnier sort, would claim the laurels if consumed in sufficient quantity.

John Evelyn apparently concurred with this estimation, though not without reservation, in his *Acetaria* of 1699, reporting that: "In general, cabbages are thought to allay Fumes and prevent intoxication: but some will have them noxious to the sight . . . but whilst the learned are not agreed about it, Theophrastus affirms the contrary and Pliny recommends the juice raw, with a little honey, for the moist and weeping eye, not the dry and the dull." It is believed that cabbage was introduced into America by the French explorer Jacques Cartier, who first planted seed in Canada in 1541.

Red or burgundy headed cabbage was known to be bred in Germany by A.D. 1150 and, according to John Gerard and his *Herball,* in Britain by 1597. Vilmorin-Andrieux in *The Vegetable Garden* of 1885 lists a total of 68 varieties of cabbage, 4 of them being of the red or ruby variety. There are only a few other denizens of the vegetable garden that can rival the ruby cabbage for sheer force of presence. 'Ruby Perfection' is a refinement of the old, immensely popular 'Ruby Ball,' with better yields, longer standing without splitting, and easier growing habits. A patch of these in the garden will absolutely entrance the eye: the heads a deep, glaucous purple 6 to 8 inches across and 2 to 3 pounds in weight, each nestled into dramatically cupped outer leaves tinged with blue.

Cabbage is a hardy, cool-season crop that does best under uniformly cool, moist conditions, so start indoors 4 weeks before last frost and plant out early, or direct sow in late June, ½ inch deep, thinned to 18 inches, to allow the heads to form during the cool of fall. Harvest the sweet, mild heads in 80 to 85 days. Make a tasty slaw out of this one with a rich, mayonnaisey, caraway-scented dressing.

Cabbage 'Ruby Perfection'

❧ 10. Cabbage 'Savoy Express' ❧
Brassica oleracea capitata

"But, after all, cabbage is greatly accus'd for lying undigested in the stomach and provoking eructations; which makes me wonder at the veneration we read the ancients had for them, calling them divine and swearing 'per brassicum.'"

—John Evelyn,
Acetaria: A Discourse of Sallets, 1699

Members of the *Brassica oleracea* family have been known to have been consumed for over 4,000 years, loose-leaved kales and mustards being thought to be the oldest varieties. Most contemporary botanists believe *Brassicas* were originally native to the Mediterranean region, although there were certainly edible, cruciferous, leafy plants growing in nearly every corner of the globe by very early on. By the first century B.C., a refining preference for large-leaved varieties with tight clusters at the center eventually led to the development of the cabbage as we know it today. This stout, dense, long-keeping, almost invincible plant was named *Brassica oleracea* var. *capitata,* or "with a head," and was so adored in ancient Egypt that it was worshipped as a god.

In ancient Rome, cabbage seemed to be a panacea for just about any physical malaise, the crushed leaves being recommended for wounds and dislocated joints, then cabbage raw for gout, cooked for warts and weak eyes, and the juice for deafness. It was broadly believed that no disease could lodge in the body of anyone who ate cabbage in quantity. The Roman invasion of Britain brought this popular cure-all to England, where, in his *Acetaria,* John Evelyn took a more circumspect tact, reporting that: "Cabbage, *Brassica* (and its several kinds) Pompey's favorite dish so highly celebrated by old Cato, Pythagorus and Chrysippus the Physician (as the only Panacea) is not so generally magnified by the rest of the doctors, as affording but a crass and melancholy juice; yet loosening if but moderately boil'd, if over-much, astringent according to C. Celsus; and therefore seldom eaten raw excepting by the Dutch."

Three types of the especially beautiful Savoy Cabbage were being grown in Germany by 1543, and these were first introduced from Savoy into England in the seventeenth century. The modern hybrid 'Savoy Express' is the variety I recommend here, though there are certainly other lovely Savoys one could recommend as well. 'Savoy Express' is particularly notable for its ability to withstand summer heat and produce exceptionally early: in about 55 days from transplant. This handsome cultivar also boasts the beautiful, heavily ruffled and crinkled leaves that make Savoys so visually distinctive, these being of a lovely dark blue-green hue with paler, sunnier centers. 'Savoy Express' is also famously firm, an excellent holder, and possessed of a wonderfully tender, sweet flavor and, for all these attractive properties, was made an All-American Selections Winner in 2000.

The small, early heads, weighing in at about 1 to 1½ pounds a piece, are perfect for a spring or fall planting in most areas of North America. Sow seed indoors about 5 or 6 weeks prior to transplanting into the garden, 12 inches apart, after threat of frost. Cabbage likes a sunny, well-drained, loam soil that's been amended with some organic matter but will do fine in even mediocre soil. However, it's important to never grow cabbage or any other *Brassica* in the same soil more than once every 3 years (and to keep soil pH above 6.8) to avoid the dreaded club root, a fungal disease of which, I assure you, you want no part. I like the lovely, crumpled heads of 'Savoy Express' cut into thick wedges, braised in chicken stock, then tossed with a dollop of sour cream and some cumin and coriander.

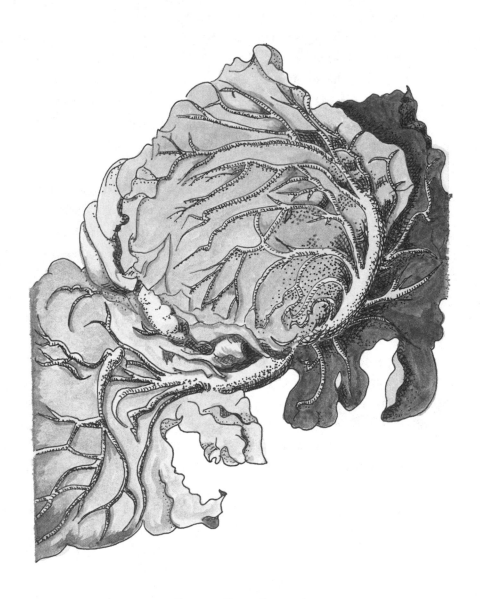

Cabbage 'Savoy Express'

CARDOON 'GIGANTE'

❧ 11. Cardoon 'Gigante' ❧
Cynara cardunculus

"Our country men are fools to serve vegetables which asses and other beasts refuse for fear of pricking their lips."

—Pliny the Elder, first century A.D.

The cardoon, also known as the "Prickly Artichoke" is certainly the wild ancestor of all members of the *Cynara* family, and as such is incredibly ancient. Its prickly presence can still be encountered growing wild all over the Argentine pampas, and it is still such a rampant nuisance in Australia it is referred to as the "Weed Artichoke." Dioscorides, botanist to the infamous Roman emperor Nero, referred to its cultivation on a large scale near Great Carthage in the first century A.D. and John Trescadant, the far-ranging English botanist and explorer, mentions seeing several acres of it being cultivated near Brussels in 1629. In Italy in the fifteenth century, the cardoon shared the same lusty reputation as its cousin the artichoke, being mentioned as "an aphrodisiac dear to Venus," and while the Greek naturalist Pliny also spoke glowingly of its medicinal virtues, he clearly shunned it as an edible plant. The Quakers ultimately delivered it to the North American continent in the late eighteenth century.

With its majestic silver-green foliage and handsome, purple, thistlelike flowers towering to an imposing 5 or 6 feet, the cardoon is an indisputably magnificent plant in the garden. Both spineless and spiny varieties of the cardoon are still cultivated, most notably the 'Cardoon de Tours' in the latter category, first mentioned in Vilmorin-Andrieux in the nineteenth century, and the 'Spanish Cardoon,' with its large solid ribs and spineless leaves, in the former. In the United States, our only seed option is frequently a generic cardoon; however, I recommend here the variety

'Gigante,' which is very large, handsome, and near spineless, and can be found in several current catalogues.

The cardoon will grow in a wide range of soils but produces best when transplants are grown and set out in spring, so sow seeds in the greenhouse in early or mid-March for transplanting out, about a yard apart, in mid-May in a deep, fertile, well-drained soil. Like artichokes, cardoons may also be propagated from stem pieces or suckers. The buds of the cardoon are too small and prickly to be edible, which allows the aesthetically inclined gardener to let them bloom prettily. With the cardoon, it is the stalks that are consumed after blanching, this being achieved by tying up and wrapping the stems in paper or cardboard in early fall to occlude light and make the stems tender. It is important to note that this task should be performed on a dry day, when the hearts are free from water, or they will certainly decay.

Harvest the stems in October or just before the first hard frost, about 3 weeks after wrapping, at which time the points of the leaves as well as the spiky edges should be cut off to where the stems are solid and blanched. Though this may sound like a lot of trouble, cardoons have a marvelously unique spicy/artichokey taste and accordingly are well worth the effort. Try them braised in an au gratin by first trimming the ends and removing the thick outer strands with a vegetable peeler. Then lay the stems in a baking dish drizzled with olive oil, sprinkle with sliced shallots, lemon juice, salt and pepper, pour in a bit of chicken stock, and braise until tender. Finally, pour a béchamel sauce over all, broil for 3 to 5 minutes until golden, and serve to wild acclaim.

❧ 12. Carrot 'Thumbelina' ❧
Daucus carota sativus

In seventeenth-century England, the Elizabethan and Stuart fashion for decorating hats, sleeves, and dresses with flowers, fruits, feathers, and the like was amusingly extended to include the feathery tops of carrots, the lacy green foliage being thought especially fetching when "coloring up" in the fall.

That sweet, crisp, bright orange "Bugs Bunny" of a vegetable we now identify as the carrot is a distant cry from the small, tough, pale-fleshed, and bitter persona of its original wild ancestor. Countless millennia old, the members of the *Daucus carota* family were not always the edible darlings they have become, the Greek naturalist and historian Pliny reporting in the first century A.D.: "There is one kind of wild pastinaca which grows spontaneously . . . . Another kind is grown either from the root transplanted or else from seed, the ground being dug to a very considerable depth for the purpose. It begins to be fit for eating at the end of the year, but it is still better at the end of two; even then, however, it preserves its strong pungent flavour, which it is found impossible to get rid of."

The truth was, the ancient Greeks and Romans rarely ate carrots, using them instead for medicinal purposes ranging from a poultice for ulcerous sores to prescription as both a stomach tonic and eyesight enhancer. Dioscorides, botanist to Nero, also writing in the first century A.D., stated: "Ye root ye thickness of a finger, a span long, sweet-smelling . . . is good for . . . ye bitings and strokes of venomous beasts . . . and . . . the leaves being beaten small with honey, and laid on, doth cleanse rapidly spreading destructive ulceration of soft tissues." Carrots were also broadly popular as a love potion with the ancient Greeks, who called the unprepossessing root *Philon* or *Philtron* from the Greek word *philo*,

CARROT 'THUMBELINA'

meaning "loving." As well, Greek legend maintains that the soldiers who hid in the famous Trojan Horse consumed lavish quantities of raw carrot in order to render their bowels inactive during confinement. What we know for certain is that the important antioxidants carrots contain can protect against heart disease, cancer, and cataracts, inhibit tumor growth, and even retard premature aging.

The carrot I recommend here is the curvaceous 'Thumbelina,' not only for its pretty, novel shape but also for its fairly unique ability to do well in heavy, rocky soil where other longer carrot varieties would certainly give up the ghost. A round Paris Market-type, 'Thumbelina' is a sprightly, bright orange orb sprouting a dainty root at the nether end and a froth of feathery greenery at the other. Although usually harvested at the ½-inch size, they will retain their crisp edibility up to the size of a golf ball and larger and are also notable for their sweet taste, crisp texture, and pleasing smoothness of skin, which is lovely as their shape makes them rather tiresome to peel. For all these sterling attributes, 'Thumbelina' was warmly received as an All-American Selections Winner in 1992.

All carrots need plenty of sun, although, as I've mentioned, 'Thumbelina' is blissfully free of the sandy, deep soil requirements of most. To start your carrot patch, either scatter seeds in a row and thin them out or plant them at the outset at 1- to 2-inch intervals in early spring, covering seed with finely sifted compost or sand. These pretty, ginger-colored globes are ready to harvest about 65 days from sowing and are sublime tossed with chopped garlic and rosemary, then roasted with some fingerling potatoes around a fowl for a nourishing fall meal.

ॐ

❧ 13. Cauliflower 'Violetta di Sicilia' ❧
Brassica oleracea botrytis

"Training is everything. Cauliflower is nothing but cabbage with a college education."

— Mark Twain

Cauliflower is an extremely intimate relative of broccoli, the two *Brassica oleracea* cousins being so incestuous as to share the same botanical variety, *botrytis,* which derives from the Greek meaning "cluster" as in a tightly held bunch of grapes. The word *cauliflower* is a marriage of the Latin *caulis* for cabbage and *floris* for flower and, as such, the intricately wrought, usually milky-fleshed cauliflower has always been considered the beauty of the *Brassica* family. Many believe its original home was the isle of Rhodes, and the oldest known reference to cauliflower dates from the sixth century B.C. Pliny the Elder wrote of them in the first century A.D. and they were known in Syria before the twelfth century A.D., an Arab botanist of that era referring to them as "flowering Syrian cabbage." By the end of the twelfth century, at least three varieties were described in Spain as recent introductions from Syria.

By the beginning of the sixteenth century, cauliflower had spread to Turkey and Egypt, then, via Malta and Crete, into the southern basin of the Mediterranean, Italy, and finally most of Europe by the end of the sixteenth century. In England, by 1586, cauliflower was enthusiastically offered for sale as "Cyprus colewort," suggesting introduction from the island of Cyprus, and English herbalist John Evelyn opined in 1699 that the best "cauly-flower . . . comes from Russia and Denmark." It was grown in France by 1600 and made its way to Haiti as early as 1565, finding its way to the New World with the earliest slave trade. By the late nineteenth century, as many as a dozen varieties of cauliflower were offered by American seed growers.

The cauliflower 'Violetta di Sicilia' is as lushly dramatic a diva as she sounds, with a deep, imperial purple 4- to 5-inch head (or "curd" as one calls the compact cluster of what are actually undeveloped flower buds), artfully framed by signature, cruciform leaves, and borne atop a handsome 2-foot-tall central stalk. Modern, purple varieties of cauliflower are the result of a purple-hued mutant discovered in a field in the late 1980s and years of classical breeding at the research facility Danefeld in Denmark. As with both red cabbages and wines, the gorgeous burgundy-violet coloration is due to anthocyanins, members of the phenolic antioxidant family, the same compounds that induce many doctors to recommend the health benefits of a glass of red wine. Equally attractive is the fact that, after you cut the main head, 'Violetta di Sicilia' will reward you with a lush crop of side shoots, resembling nothing so much as sprigs of Purple Sprouting Broccoli.

All crucifers are cool-weather vegetables, and cauliflower is more sensitive to hot weather than broccoli, so it will do best when daytime temperatures are between 65 and 80 degrees and it's set out as a 4- to 6-week-old transplant rather than planted from seed. 'Violetta di Sicilia' will grow well in any reasonably fertile, well-drained soil, and is frost tolerant so, for a fall crop, set out transplants around July 1, spaced 14 to 20 inches apart. Harvest the curds before the buds begin to separate, about 2 months after transplant, cutting each head so that at least two wrapper leaves are present for optimum flavor. I've always thought the sweet, nutty flavor of cauliflower is wonderfully enhanced as they prepare it in India: simmered with potato, onion, and broth into a fragrant and savory vegetable curry.

CAULIFLOWER 'VIOLETTA DI SICILIA'

❧ 14. Cayenne Pepper ❧
Capsicum annuum

In 1550, the alarmist and acutely culinarily timid Flemish botanist and physician Rembert Dodoens announced that the hot peppers recently introduced into Europe were strong enough to kill dogs.

The plain fact is that hot peppers are not "peppers" at all. They are actually members of the *capsicum* family and the fruit is technically a berry. This misnomer traces back to Christopher Columbus himself, who believed he had found an alternative source for the highly valued spice *Piper nigrum* or black pepper, native to India. Although cayenne pepper is native to tropical America alone, it is now cultivated in tropical locations throughout the world, particularly southeast Asia, China, southern Italy, and Mexico. Thomas Jefferson first planted Cayenne Peppers in 1767 at Shadwell, his birthplace, on the eve of his twenty-fourth birthday.

Since ancient times, hot peppers, both fresh and dried, have also been used by healers to cure a virtual panoply of ailments, from joint pain to yellow fever. The American Medical Association still recommends ten drops of hot pepper sauce in half a glass of water as an extremely effective sore throat remedy and most herbalists will choose hot pepper powder over any other single medicinal herb. The first North American to advocate hot pepper in healing is believed to have been Samuel Thomson, creator of Thomsonian herbal medicine, a brand of pharmacology that enjoyed considerable popularity before the Civil War. Thomson believed most disease was caused by cold and cured by heat, so he prescribed "warming" herbs almost exclusively. After the Civil War, Cayenne Pepper in particular was recommended for everything from arthritis and muscle soreness to cough, fever, nausea, and toothache. Recently, ingested Cayenne has been shown to possess substantial pain-relieving properties for certain kinds of chronic pain, and it is a fact that a teaspoon of

Cayenne in hot water will stop a heart attack in progress. In the end, a very handy plant to have around.

As if all this medicinal distinction is not recommendation enough, the Cayenne is also a very pretty plant indeed. Its glossy, curling, brilliantly carmine "horns" hang copiously from handsome, bushy plants that grow to a height of 3 feet or more, and this exceedingly attractive show is further enhanced by dainty, drooping, white to yellow flowers that will bloom for a good part of the summer. This, in fact, is a plant so handsome that I would consider it for a container garden as well, for a single plant will not only beautify your deck or terrace but supply you with a surprising abundance of fruit for all your herbal and culinary needs. Cayennes are also perfect peppers for drying: just pull a needle and thread through their green "caps," hang in a decorative *ristra* to dry, and make use of them all winter, too.

Peppers are definitely tropicals and need to be treated with warm attention. Start them in the greenhouse or your sunniest window 6 weeks before your frost date and don't plant out till June. Space them about 18 inches apart in a nice, sunny aspect in your garden and just watch them perform. Peppers are surprisingly carefree plants as they provide their own pest deterrent: when one attempts to bite into them, they definitely "bite" back. The pods of the cayenne can be pickled and used in pepper sauce and salsa as well as dried. To make a simply splendid remedy for a sore throat, mix a teaspoon of dried cayenne with two of honey in your homiest mug, fill with hot water, and sip soothingly.

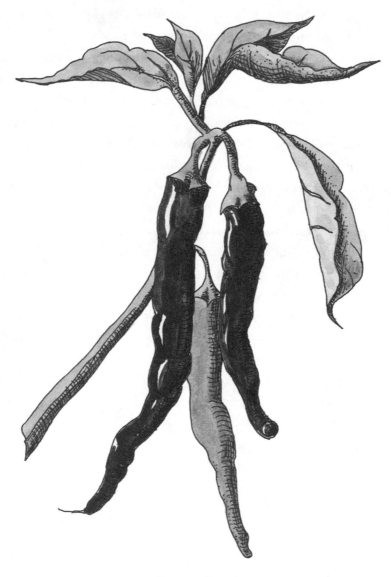

CAYENNE PEPPER

CELERIAC

❧ 15. Celeriac ❧
Apium graveolens rapaceum

Celery has maintained a long history as an aphrodisiac, the women of ancient Rome consuming it in surprising quantity to inflame their libidos, and the famously soigné Mme. De Maintenon making "soupe de celeri" an integral part of the intimate dinners she held at the court of Louis IV.

Celeriac (var. *rapaceum*) developed from the same wild species as did stalk celery (*Apium graveolens*) in the Mediterranean basin and was in medicinal and religious use, chiefly for its bitter stalks, in the early history of some of our greatest civilizations, including those of Egypt, Greece, and Italy. The Greeks called it *selinon* and it is mentioned in Homer's *Odyssey* in 850 B.C., but Celeriac didn't really achieve importance as a vegetable plant until the Middle Ages, Italian and Swiss botanists giving the first descriptions of it in about 1600. Celeriac was first recorded as a food plant in France in 1623, and was commonly cultivated in most of Europe by the end of the seventeenth century. Oddly, it is still considered rather a curiosity in England and is virtually unknown in this country.

Also known as celery root, knob celery, and turnip-rooted celery, Celeriac is cousin to anise, carrots, parsley, and parsnips, some of these being bred for their edible stalks and tops, the others for their edible roots. Basically, Celeriac is a celery variety refined over time to form an increasingly large, solid, globular "root" just below the soil surface. Unlike stalk celery, the roots are eaten cooked, never raw, and taste like a marvelously subtle blend of celery and parsley. It is unfathomable to me that so delicious, wonderfully hearty, eminently storable a winter vegetable, which also makes a boldly verdant show in the garden, should go so unrecognized in the "try anything" United States. Additionally, half a cup of Celeriac contains only thirty calories and no cholesterol or fat, and provides an excellent source of dietary fiber.

Because of its relative obscurity, Celeriac is only rarely discussed by cultivar, 'Large Prague' being the commonest variety available but also, happily, the most stately in terms of size and vigorous in terms of cultivation. Admittedly, 'Large Prague' as well as other Celeriacs do have a couple of slight drawbacks, one being their rather long growing season (112 days), the other their, well . . . physical oddity. Above ground, this truly underrated vegetable offers up a gorgeously symmetrical crown of green, celery-like growth sprouting sputnick-style to 12 inches. However, pull up this pretty, green crown and what you unearth looks like, well . . . a troll-like ball of roots about sums it up. Do not let these incidentals dissuade you.

Celeriac typically takes about 6 months from seeding to maturity, although the root is edible at any earlier stage; in any case, start seeds indoors 3 months before your frost date. Germination can be quite long (3 or 4 weeks), so be patient. Transplant out just after last frost 10 inches apart, and do your utmost to keep this particular patch well watered as Celeriac loves a moist soil — a good layer of mulch will help you tremendously in this regard as well. Harvest the roots when baseball-sized and, just as with the Frog Prince, when you pare off the warty exterior, you will magically reveal the enchanting pale flesh within. I advise boiling and mashing these with half as much peeled potato, then whisking roughly with a knob of butter, a lashing of cream, a pinch of salt, and a drizzle of truffle oil. Toss some crisp-fried apple bits on top at your own peril.

❧ 16. Chard 'Bright Lights' ❧
Beta vulgaris cicla

"It grew with me in 1596 . . . which plant nature doth seeme to play and sport herselfe: for the seeds taken from the plant, which was altogether of one colour and sowne, doth bring forth plants of many and variable colours . . ."

—John Gerard, *The Herball* or
General History of Plantes, 1636

L et's get the Swiss-ness issue out and over, once and for all. The hard fact is, chard isn't any more native to Switzerland than, say, the palm tree. Clocks, yes. Intractable neutrality, surely. But chard? Not on your retentive timetable. An erstwhile theory has it that the Swiss botanist Koch was the author of this cultivar's scientific name and, since that auspicious moment, its name has honored his homeland. In truth, the original home of chard most probably lies considerably farther south in the Mediterranean region, as its culinary and medicinal virtues were lauded by Aristotle himself as early as the fourth century B.C.

A member of the *Beta vulgaris* family, chard is a distant cousin of those other "greens" spinach and orach, and a kissing cousin of the beet, the latter historically cultivated for its root as the former has been for its tasty and succulent, above-ground midribs and leaves. The English herbalist John Gerard continued to note of chard in his *Herball* of 1636 that "the leaves . . . are for the most part very broad and thicke, like the middle part of the cabbage leafe, which is equal in goodnesse with the leaves of the cabbage being boyled." Chard, historically, has been available in a number of color variations since its first herbal documentations, the Swiss botanist Casper Bauhin recording white, yellow, red, and "dark" varieties in his *Phytopinax* of 1596.

'Bright Lights,' a refined strain of Five Color Silverbeet, is actually a collection of a number of chards cultivated for their coloration by

CHARD 'BRIGHT LIGHTS'

amateur grower John Eaton in New Zealand in the mid-1990s. A 1998 All-American Selections Gold Medal Winner, 'Bright Lights' is a true showstopper in the garden. The lushly savoyed and blistered green leaves of each seedling are shot through with veins and midribs of brilliant red or orange or yellow, each combination almost neon in its vibrancy, and certainly electric as an aggregate.

Chard is also one of the healthiest vegetables on earth. A single cup of cooked chard contains 388.9 percent of your daily dose of vitamin K (important for maintaining bone health), 137.3 percent of your allotment of vitamin A, 47 percent of magnesium, and 10.2 percent of your daily dose of calcium, yet contains a paltry thirty-five calories. Its fortifying combination of nutrients and fiber also seems particularly effective in preventing digestive-tract cancers, precancerous lesions in animals having been found to be significantly reduced following diets heavy in chard extracts.

Chards are a relatively carefree thing to grow. Start in seed cups 4 weeks before last frost and plant out, or direct sow after danger of frost ½ inch deep, 2 to 3 inches apart, in well dug, fertile soil (optimum soil temperature for germination is 55 to 75 degrees). Thin to 8 to 10 inches apart after plants reach a height of 3 inches, and enjoy the show. I'm very fond of making a summer relish with the colorful midribs of these beauties (reserve the leaves to sauté as spinach). Cut stems into medium dice, sauté in a bit of olive oil with diced onion, golden raisins, a minced garlic clove, and a pinch each of brown sugar, cumin, and cardoman, toss with freshly chopped mint, cool, and enjoy.

🕸 17. Chinese Rat Tail Radish 🕸
Raphanus caudatus

"Radishes . . . are eaten alone with Salt only, as carrying their Peper in them, and were indeed by Dioscorides and Pliny celebrated above all roots whatsoever; insomuch as in the Delphic Temple . . . there was Raphanus ex auro discatus, a Radish of solid Gold; and 'tis said of Moschius that he wrote a whole volume in their praise."

— John Evelyn, *Acetaria: A Discourse of Sallets,* 1699

A ctually a member of the mustard family grown for its root rather than for its leafy greens or seeds, "radish" derives from the Latin *radix,* meaning "root" and, in its wildest form is indistinguishable from the ancient charlock or wild mustard. Radishes have been under cultivation in China for so many thousands of years that most botanists believe they must have originated there, although they are impressively ancient to other countries as well. For instance, radishes have been eaten in Egypt literally from the beginning of that civilization and were frequently depicted in tomb paintings. The Romans were known to be cultivating radishes at the beginning of the Christian era, and renderings of radishes having been unearthed from the ruins of Pompeii.

Greek writers of the first century A.D., including Dioscorides and Pliny the Elder, made frequent mention of radishes, and the Greeks esteemed the radish so highly that small, solid gold replicas of them were placed in Apollonian temples as objects of devotion, while beets and turnips, used for other deific offerings, had to be content with replication in the baser metals of silver and lead. Radishes were known to be growing throughout southern Europe by the thirteenth century A.D., although for herbal and medicinal purposes only. The first culinary reference to the radish occurs in the sixteenth century, which is when the radish reached England as well, and by 1629 radishes were being cultivated by the New World colonists of Massachusetts.

Native to South Asia, the Chinese Rat Tail Radish, also known as the Javan and Serpent-Tailed Radish, while clearly a member of the *Raphanus* family, is unlike any radish you've ever seen. First of all, it's not this plant's root you eat, but rather its green, elegantly tapered seedpods, which look, well, like a rat or serpent's tail. For some reason, this charming edible plant's cultivation seems once again limited to the Far East, which is really a pity, and I urge all vegetable gardeners to search out this really unusual cultivar. The prettily formed, crisp, deliciously edible, 6- to 12-inch-long pods, borne on arching canes to 3 feet, are often tinged with a lovely blush of purple. As well, the graceful, leafy branches fairly bristle with them, and a patch of this exotic beauty will also offer to the adventurous gardener the additional glamour of a flurry of pretty white to violet blossoms in midsummer.

Chinese Rat Tail Radish seed should be directly and thinly sown when soil temperatures have hit 60 degrees. Thin to about 6 inches apart, which will result in a thicket of this intriguing Asian food plant, and harvest the first pods about fifty days from sowing. The Chinese Rat Tail Radish enjoyed a brief European culinary vogue in the nineteenth century, when it was described in Vilmorin-Andrieux's *The Vegetable Garden* and pioneered in Europe by the French seedsmen Pailleux & Bois. The edible pods, best picked when young, are milder than most root radishes and can be used in the same way. They are wonderful eaten whole and raw, excellent chopped into salads, and will surely dazzle your dinner guests with their unique history, form, and flavor.

Chinese Rat Tail Radish

❧ 18. Chiogga Beet ❧
Beta vulgaris

"The great and beautiful Beet . . . is not only pleasant to the taste but also delightful to the eie."

—John Gerard, *The Herball* or
General History of Plantes, 1636

Beets are members of the *Chenopodiaceae* or Goosefoot family (so called because some of its most visible members bear leaves thought by some early and visually imaginative horticulturists to resemble the foot of a goose) and as such are related to the Spinaches, the South American grain Quinoa, common Lamb's Quarter, and good old Good King Henry (or *bonus Henricus* as they say in Latin). The species to which beets belong, *Beta vulgaris,* comes in three basic sub-species: *vulgaris*, the familiar red or golden Beetroot, including the Sugar Beet (var. *attissima*); *cicla,* which are the Leaf Beets and Chards; and *maritima,* the Sea Beet, which is most probably the wild and wooly ancestor of the lot.

Beets are believed to have originated in southern Europe and North Africa around the Mediterranean basin, being known in Italy from about A.D. 300. From Italy, they journeyed north and west to the rest of Europe, where they became commonly known as "Roman" beets. They were stock fare on German tables by the thirteenth century and had reached broad popularity in Turkey by the fifteenth. However, the beet as we know it today is a relatively modern invention, as ancient beetroots were of the long, turnipy variety, the round root with which we are familiar having been developed at Castelnaudary in the Languedoc region of France in the early nineteenth century.

Beet cultivars come in a broad variety of colors and shapes, from red and purple to gold and white, round, oval, and cylindrical. The startling

Chioggia Beet was first introduced to American gardeners in the late 1840s from the charming fishing town of the same name on the Adriatic coast of Italy. In truth, aboveground, it is a fairly pedestrian plant with certainly attractive but not notable green foliage. And even when plucked from the earth, it's a fairly standard sort of red beet. But cut into it and be prepared for a bit of op art magic from Mother Nature, as the flesh of the Chiogga is really uniquely beautiful, boasting surprising, alternating rings of crisp red-pink and white, exactly resembling a bull's-eye.

Beets are hearty creatures and can even withstand temperatures below freezing, so direct sow this one in early spring as soon as you can work the soil, optimally when soil warms to 45 degrees and air temperature to 50 degrees. Although some avow beets will tolerate part shade, I'm of the experience that they require full sun and will not make good roots without it. As with all root crops, a well-turned soil is essential and a light, sandy loam ideal, permitting the longed for, rapid, uninterrupted growth of roots: in heavy or poorly drained soils, you might even consider preparing a raised bed for them. Space plants 2 to 4 inches apart, then thin them to 4 to 6 inches when plants are 2 to 3 inches tall.

You can expect to harvest anywhere from 56 to 70 days after sowing, and you can clip the greens in just 30 to 45 days (these tops possess a particularly fine flavor). Chioggas have a wonderfully sweet taste, so how about employing them in a zingy Asian broth by swirling some mashed anchovies into a ginger- and lemon-scented stock, then tossing in some thinly sliced Chioggas and green onion tops as both decoration and crisp, tangy complement?

CHIOGGA BEET

❧ 19. Crimson Forest Onion ❧
Allium fistulosum

"Onions make a man wink, drink and stink."

— Old English Proverb

Onions are so ancient to so many parts of the globe that their origins are somewhat obscure, although most botanists believe them to be originally native to either Asia or the Middle East. Onions were cultivated in Chinese gardens as early as the third millennium B.C., were noted in the most ancient Vedic writings of India, and can be traced back to 3500 B.C. in Egypt, where they were sacred objects of worship. Additionally, in what was ancient Mesopotamia, archeologists have unearthed a Sumerian inscription dating to 2400 B.C. that relates, in an apparently kindly showing from the gods: "The oxen of the gods plowed the city governor's onion patches." However, from all evidence, it was the Egyptians who were paranormally wild about the onion, among other practices seeing fit to stuff virtually every orifice a mummy offered with a bulb of two before entombment.

Many Egyptologists believe this interesting obsession was born of the ancient Egyptian view that the onion, with its circle-within-a-circle configuration, was a symbol of eternal life. In various mummies, onions have been found adorning the pelvic and thoracic cavities and lying flattened against the ears, and King Ramses IV himself, when he died in 1160 B.C., was entombed with onions filling his eye sockets. A bit later in history, onions were so esteemed by the Emperor Charlemagne and France that they were accepted as a form of payment and even written into French feudal deeds. By the Middle Ages the three main vegetable staples on any European table were beans, cabbages, and onions. Onions found their way to the New World through Haiti with Columbus, although by 1493 strains of wild onions could already be found growing throughout North America.

There are hundreds of varieties of onions, but here we will describe a pretty member of the *fistulosum* or "bunching onion" family, so called because, scallion or leeklike, they are grown for their edible stalks rather than their bulbs and, when grown perennially, will set in bunches. This ancient Asian cultivar is usually of a standard-issue green leaf portion and white stalk, but here I recommend to you a bunching onion of a very different color: the beautiful specimen Crimson Forest. The Crimson Forest boasts gorgeous deep ruby-hued bulblets and necks, the color extending to three or four layers and gradating dramatically to handsome green tops. In contrast to a hefty red bulb onion (*Allium cepa*), say a Wethersfield, there is something ineffably elegant and graceful about a bunch of Crimson Forest Onions, which is another excellent reason to commend them to you here.

Crimson Forest Onions are cultivated in much the same way as the leek, and also share a longish growing period of about 120 days from sowing. Therefore, start indoors or in very early spring for a fall crop, or in the fall for a crop the following spring. You may seed thickly as bunching onions only need a couple of inches of growing space each, and plants can be harvested at any stage. Like leeks, bunching onions are also extremely cold hearty and will overwinter in many American temperature zones. Additionally, when used like scallions, some harvested and some allowed to develop, the plants left to multiply will each have half a dozen or so divisions the next year (thus "bunching"). Crimson Forest's enchanting, glossy scarlet bulblets are also very tender and well flavored, so why not include them, parboiled to lose a bit of astringency, on your next crudité platter?

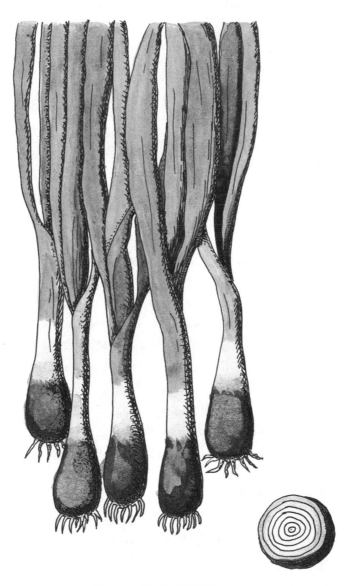

CRIMSON FOREST ONION

❦ 20. d'Algers Melon ❦
Cucumis melo

"Melon, Melo, to have been reckon'd rather among fruits and tho' an usual ingredient in our sallet yet for its transcendent delicacy and flavor, cooling and exhilarating nature (if sweet, dry, weighty, and well-fed) not only superior to the gourd-kind but paragon with the noblest productions of the garden."

— John Evelyn, *Acetaria: A Discourse of Sallets,* 1699

I am stretching the boundaries of this tome to its elastic limit in including four varieties of melon, my rationale for this bold move being that, as a member of the *Curcurbitae* family, the melon is, for all intents and purposes, merely a cucumber or squash with a somewhat sweeter deportment. A clan of delicious diversity, melons can range from olive-sized to a Guinness Record-holding 226 pounds, and run the physical gamut from white to yellow, red, and blue, and from satin-skinned to wrinkled, striped, netted, ribbed, warted, and freckled. They were under cultivation in Africa and Asia 4,000 years ago; in 1973 the perfectly preserved body of the Chinese Marquise of Tai, dating to the second century B.C., was discovered in the province of Hunam, with melon seeds still in her stomach.

Melons probably entered the Mediterranean with Arabs and Moors bound for settlement in the Andalusia by the last century B.C., and several varieties were grown by the early Romans and Greeks, both Pliny and Columella singing their gastronomic praises, and Apicius including several melon recipes in his *De Re Coquinaria.* In the twelfth century, Marco Polo, traveling through Afghanistan on his way to China, reported finding "the best melons in the world in very great quantity." Melons were introduced to the New World on Columbus's second voyage in 1493, described by John Gerard in England in 1597, and under extensive cultivation in France by 1629. Wild varieties of *Cucumis melo* can still be found growing in the deserts of Africa, Arabia, Asia, and Australia.

The beautiful d'Algers Melon, a variety of cantaloupe, is an ancient French heirloom thought to have originated in Algiers (thus its common name), and was most probably carried into Andalusia by the Moors. Described as notably "sweet and good" in Vilmorin-Andrieux's *Les Plantes Potageres* of 1883, d'Algers is a truly magnificent melon, as intricately carved as a precious gem with ten elegant ribs cutting through it latitudinally. Its beautiful reticulated surface, which will move through several pretty shades of orange before it achieves its final coloration, is sutured like a pumpkin, with clouds of raised green "galls" skittering across its delicately mottled surface. In French, members of the *Cucumis melo* family with this kind of graceful reticulation are charmingly called *melons brodis,* or "embroidered" melons, this pretty example also boasting equally attractive, deep green, palmately lobed leaves and a heavenly fragrance that will literally perfume a room.

A French poet once said, "There are three things which cannot support mediocrity: poetry, wine, and melons." To grow to perfection, the melon requires uniformly warm temperatures over a longish, 3-month growing period. Therefore, transplant 4-week-old seedlings into well-manured hills after soil is warmed to at least 60 degrees. Many serious growers raise melons on black plastic because of the additional warmth it provides: although this method is wildly effective, I, personally, am unwilling to sacrifice so much aesthetic integrity to yield. The pale orange flesh of this handsome brute, while thin in relation to other melons, is delightfully sweet, so how about blending it up into a refreshing summer soup with some orange juice, a squeeze of lime, and a handful of fresh, finely chopped mint?

d'Algers Melon

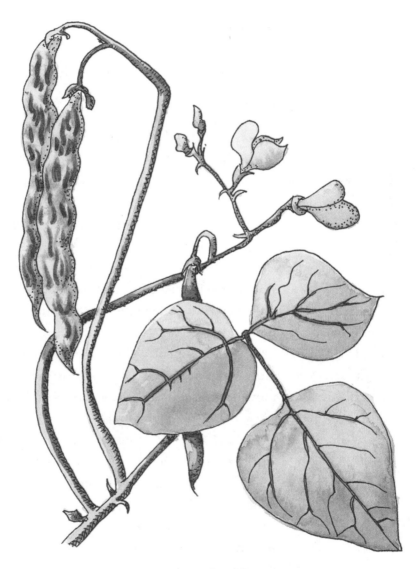

Dragon Tongue Bush Bean

❧ 21. Dragon Tongue Bush Bean ❧
Phaseolus vulgaris

The "green" bean or haricot vert, also widely known as the "French bean" as it came into England by way of the Huguenots during the reign of Elizabeth I, is in fact an American native introduced by the Spanish into Europe in the sixteenth century.

I had always assumed that with a name as exotic as "Dragon Tongue," bespeaking flaming nostrils, flashing scales, and a likeness picked out on silk in thread of gold, this bean must surely be an ancient Asian heirloom. Not at all. In fact, this lovely bush bean, which also goes by the equally exotic names "Dragon Langerie" and "Merveille de Piemente," is actually a Dutch variety dating from the nineteenth century. It is also interesting to note that cultivated green beans of the bush variety, like this one, only really came into their own in the early nineteenth century (until the eighteenth century, all cultivated green beans grown on the European continent were of the vining or pole variety). However, on their native American continent, it is known that, historically, the North American Indians grew green beans both of the "walking" (vining) and "not walking" (bush) varieties.

Let's also clear up once and for all this idea of the "green" bean. Green beans (*Phaseolus vulgaris* versus broad or fava beans, var. *Vicia faba*), originated in the Americas and were only brought to Europe by the Spanish in the sixteenth century. Green beans can actually be myriad colors, from burgundy to brilliant yellow and everywhere in between. They were called green as they were eaten green, i.e. when young with pod and all, to distinguish them from the native European beans (*Vicia faba*), which were only eaten dried or shelled. Additionally, "green" beans of any color can be either of the pole (vining and climbing) or bush (compact, low-growing habit) variety. As for haricots verts, this gastronomical designation has come to describe the thinnest possible "green" beans that are actually green.

Bush beans are some of the prettiest vegetables on earth but they are somewhat shy in displaying their attractions as they prefer to hide their charms pendulously beneath their rather pedestrian green foliage. But one has only to poke through that green overcanopy to discover bundles of pretty fruit of countless colors and description. The Dragon Tongue is truly one of the loveliest, with its purple, flamelike markings mottled over creamy yellow, Romano-type pods. Both the yield and the intense, beany flavor of the flat, 5-inch-long fruit are remarkably good and they're equally suited for use as a fresh snap bean when young, or as a shelled bean when fully mature.

As a snap bean, harvest when the pods turn from lime green to yellow and purple. If dried beans are desired, let the pods dry on the vine, then split and harvest. Direct sow seeds when temperatures are well warmed up 2 to 3 inches apart and 1 inch deep in rows 18 inches to 36 inches apart. Because of their shallow root growth, beans require careful watering and will use up to ¼ inch of water a day during hot weather. Expect sturdy, compact, 24-inches-tall plants in 55 to 60 days. Dragon Tongue beans can be used in any green bean recipe but, as in all things culinary, particularly fresh produce, simplicity is best. In my opinion, beans are optimally prepared when they are steamed briefly, drained and refreshed, then tossed with a knob of butter, a shake of salt and pepper, a sprinkle of lemon juice, and a handful of fresh, chopped herb like tarragon, basil, or mint.

❦ 22. Dwarf Blue Curled Scotch Kale ❦
Brassica oleracea acephala

Kale's botanical name Brassica oleracea acephala *translates roughly to "many-armed smelling thing without a head," which may be one of the reasons this particular food plant never made prom committee in high school.*

It was probably well over 3,000 years ago that the first wild "cabbages" grew on the windswept cliffs of England and Scotland, scavenged by the nomadic tribes that drifted through, driven alternately by war and the promise of better foraging. By as early as 500 B.C., the tribes' general preference for increasingly larger- or denser-leaved varieties had led to the development of the cruciferous-leaved "cole" crops we know today. These coleworts included what we now know as cabbage, cauliflower, broccoli, Brussels sprouts, kale, kohlrabi, cress, and mustard, the original "colewort" of Middle English ultimately being corrupted to the "collard" so dear to the American South. These incredibly hardy cultivars, truly defining frost tolerance, have been mainstays in sustaining human culture for centuries.

Also known historically as borecale, coolstock, greenwort, and ragged jack, kale is believed by some to be the original antecedent of the rest of the *Brassica* clan, as well as one of the most nutritious of garden vegetables, being uncommonly rich in calcium, folic acid, and vitamins A and C. As recently as a century ago, before the advent of refrigeration, kale was a practically universal cold-season staple: cattle had their own proprietary varieties and even chickens thrived on it. In many parts of Great Britain and northern Europe, kale is still grown extensively as an important winter crop, the two main types being the Scotch group, which has curly leaves, and the Siberian group, which includes the Red Russian varieties.

Kale is currently a much undervalued crop in my opinion, legendary for its hardiness when all else is failing and its considerable health

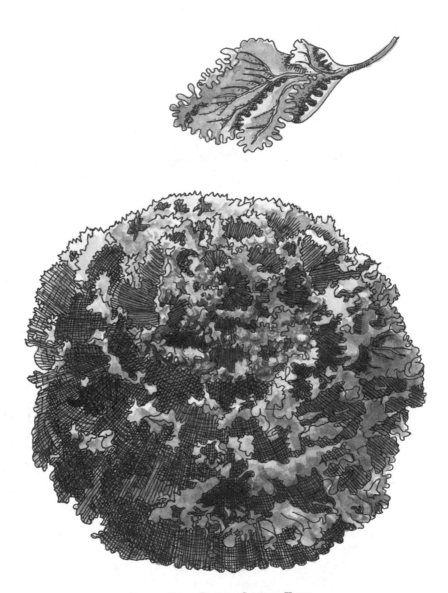

DWARF BLUE CURLED SCOTCH KALE

benefits, but fairly ignored by gastronomes and other elevated palates. Kale's wonderful diversity, handsome physical presence, nutritive value, and excellent taste should make it a far more popular garden vegetable than it is today. There are types suited to literally every North American clime with a coolish growing season, from summer in Alaska to winter in Florida, and if you're lucky enough to live in an area that is U.S. Hardiness Zone 6b or milder, you'll have the added luxury of gathering sweet, tender new shoots in spring.

Dwarf Blue Curled Scotch Kale, the most widely grown kale in the United States, was developed in 1950 at the Virginia Truck Experiment Station from the heirloom variety "Dwarf Green Curled," which had been helping set edible kale standards (green, frilly, upright leaves) since before 1865. Introduced initially as "Vates Dwarf Blue Curled Scotch," this is a compact but lushly handsome, truly blue star in the vegetable garden. The uniformly low-growing plants boast frilly, finely curled, very blue-green leaves on 1-foot-tall plants, which stand well and maintain color superbly. As with all kales, a frost improves sweetness, and this type is known to be so especially hardy that many find it will overwinter with a modicum of mulching, even in the North.

In the Northeast, we sow indoors just after the Fourth of July so that the seedlings are 3 to 4 weeks old at transplanting in mid-August. You can expect maturation in 50 to 70 days, so adjust the timetable to suit your best estimate of a fall frost date, spacing plants 14 inches apart at transplant. Try these tender, sweet, frost-nipped leaves in a quick and brightly savory stir-fry with some slivered pork, ginger, garlic, and a splash of soy sauce.

❦ 23. Early Purple Vienna Kohlrabi ❦
Brassica oleracea caulorapa

In A.D. 43, when the Holy Roman Emperor Claudius sent his general Aulus Plautus and 20,000 men to take Britain from the sons of King Cymbeline, the Roman army carried not only swords but seeds to feed themselves, and effectively introduced cabbages and turnips into northern Europe.

The ancient coleworts were as diversely domesticated a plant group as any on earth, with some, like kales and collards, being refined for their stems and leaves, and others, like cabbages and sprouts, being selected for their tight, compact heads, while still others, like broccoli and cauliflower, were bred for their unopened flower buds. The *Brassica* variety Kohlrabi was probably first developed near modern Germany, when kale plants with short, fleshy stems started to be selected, resulting in the cultivar we now know as *Brassica oleracea* var. *caulorapa, caulorapa* translating to "stem turnip." Kohlrabi as a named food crop was known to exist in the Mediterranean as early as the first century A.D., having been noted by Pliny as the "Corinthian Turnip," a designation apparently derived from their abundant growth near the city of Corinth, and listed by Apicius, author of the first known cookbook, during the same period.

Charlemagne ordered Kohlrabi to be grown in the lands under his reign in A.D. 800, although it is interesting to note that while we usually connect Charlemagne with France, his capital actually resided near Aix-la-Chapelle, now Aachen, in the western portion of Germany, which accounts for Kohlrabi's current German appellation. Kohlrabi has been in common use throughout Italy, France, and Germany from Charlemagne's era up to the present, and found its way as far afield as Israel and Africa, as well as northern India, by the seventeenth century, where it became as important to the Hindu diet as rice and greens.

For those uninitiated to the visual and culinary charms of Kohlrabi, it is more turnip than cabbage or kale: a globular, turnip-shaped bulb, riding on top of the soil rather than beneath it, and radiating a host of straight architectural stems topped with a cockade of broccoli-like leaves. Because its stem is swollen to the extreme, Kohlrabi is often mistaken for a root vegetable, thus all the "turnip" references in its past. There is a common apple-green variety, but here we recommend the far more colorful and dramatic cultivar Early Purple Vienna, a gregarious Austrian heirloom and a true joy in the garden. The bulb of Early Purple Vienna is a bright, almost iridescent deep burgundy, with its signature prickling of long, purple, radiating stems making a fine contrast to its leaves, which are of a rich, glaucous, *Brassica* blue. Interiorly, this striking crucifer is equally lovely, with sumptuous, almost ivory-colored, pale green flesh, and I can assure you that you will be hard-pressed to find a more unusual or more commented upon vegetable in the garden.

Start Early Purple Vienna Kohlrabi indoors 3 or 4 weeks before your frost date, then plant out after danger of frost 15 inches apart in fertile soil. Expect to start harvesting 75 to 100 days from transplant. The entire vegetable, low in calories and high in vitamins A and C, potassium, and calcium, is edible raw or cooked, the young, 1½- to 2-inch bulbs being optimal in flavor and texture. Do enjoy these peeled, sliced into sticks and raw, but also chunked, boiled briefly with a bit of salt, drained, then sautéed till nicely combined with a knob of butter, a diced shallot, and a splash of balsamic vinegar.

ॐ

EARLY PURPLE VIENNA KOHLRABI

❧ 24. Eggplant 'Neon' ❧
Solanum melongena

"I think of the hundreds of poems of the eggplant
& my friends who have fallen in love
over an eggplant,
who have opened the eggplant together
& swum in its seeds,
who have clung in the egg of the eggplant
& have rocked to sleep
in love's dark purple boat."

— Erica Jong, *The Eggplant Epithalamion*

Due to its membership in the highly suspect *Solanum* family as well as the bitter taste of its earliest incarnations, the eggplant has, historically, been one of those vegetables forced to wage a long and arduous battle towards gastronomic acceptance. However, by the third century A.D., its culinary competence was at least being entertained by the Chinese, and certainly the Chinese had begun the development of their signature long, thin, mild and tasty cultivars, although, bizarrely, for many years it was thought that the eggplant was only safe to ingest if prepared by professional chefs. Exactly what training prepared these experts to deal with the "madde apple" is a matter of speculation, although the eggplant's earliest Chinese designation *ch'ieh-pzu,* signifying near poisonousness, must surely place it in the same sketchy category as that other erstwhile Eastern delicacy, the blowfish. Far Eastern lore also maintains that the first Occidental to sample the eggplant consumed it raw and fell instantly into a gastric fit.

The eggplant made that familiar journey north and west along the spice roads to Spain in the twelfth century, where four varieties of this controversial plant were grown by the Spanish Moor Ibn-al-awam. The eggplant was then introduced into France by that great gastronome Louis XIV, where it enjoyed fairly wide culinary success, although it seems to have retained some of its "madde" associations and was still listed by Carl Linnaeus as late as 1753 as *Solanum insanum.* Thomas Jefferson is often credited with introducing the eggplant to the Americas, but more likely its arrival occurred on the southern coast of the Americas via slave ships in the late sixteenth century, where it became known as "Guinea Squash."

'Neon,' a twentieth-century hybrid and descendant of the earliest long, thin, Far Eastern varieties, is perhaps the most striking Asian-type eggplant available on the market. Its nearly cylindrical fruits are about 8 inches long and several in diameter, and are possessed of the most stunning, glossy, truly neon, pink-purple coloration. These gorgeously gregarious, rose-lavender fruit, crowned with bright green calyxs, are borne on handsome, bushy plants to 36 inches tall, also achieving the added commendation of pure white flesh, which is exceptionally tender, mild, and nearly seedless.

Eggplants are desperate lovers of warm temperatures and grow best in full sun, so wait until nighttime temperatures are consistently above 60 degrees before transplanting outdoors in the spring. Regular watering will help avoid bitter-tasting fruit and repeated harvesting will stimulate continuous fruit production. At harvest, the skin of an eggplant should be taut and shiny: fruit that has lost its shine and begun to change color (usually from purple to a bronzey tone) is overripe and most likely bitter. A good rule of thumb is if you press the fruit with your finger and the skin springs back, then the eggplant is ready for picking. Why not try 'Neon' in a genuine Thai-style red curry, sautéed with a dollop of red curry paste, a can of coconut milk, and some cubed, boneless chicken, then served atop some fragrant jasmine rice with chopped cilantro to garnish?

ও

EGGPLANT 'NEON'

EGYPTIAN WALKING ONION

❧ 25. Egyptian Walking Onion ❧
Allium cepa

"How this noble bulb was deified in Egypt we are told, and that whilst they were building the pyramids there was spent on this root ninety tun of gold among the workmen. So luscious and tempting it seems they were that as whole nations have subsisted on them alone, so the Israelites were ready to return to slavery and brick-making for the love of them."

—John Evelyn, *Acetaria: A Discourse of Sallets*, 1699

Although the very first onions consumed by our ancestors in our prehistory were undoubtedly of the wild and foraged variety, many botanists also believe onions constitute one of the earliest of domesticated crops. This popular early vegetable was cultivated in the gardens of the ancient kings of both Ur and Babylon as early as 2100 B.C., and appears in tomb paintings of both the Old and New Kingdoms of Egypt. Some historians theorize that aside from their metaphysical significance, onions were also so highly esteemed by the Egyptians because their strong scent was believed capable of inducing the dead to breathe again. Others believe this plant was virtually worshipped due to the onion's strong antiseptic properties, which would undoubtedly come in handy in the sanitarily vague afterlife.

In India, as early as the sixth century B.C., the famous herbal treatise *Charaka-Sanhita* celebrates the onion as good for the heart, the eyes, and the joints, and Pliny, in the first century A.D., advocated the onion for mouth sores, dog bites, and toothache. Additionally, the athletes of the Greek Olympiad used onions to fortify themselves for the games and would consume vast quantities of them juiced, raw, or boiled, and, exteriorly, slather their bodies with poultices of onion to strengthen them. By the Middle Ages, onions were so highly regarded throughout the

Old World that they were often accepted as rent payment and given as wedding gifts.

The Egyptian Walking Onion, also called the Egyptian Tree Onion, is a really fascinating variety. An ancient type of scallion, it is thought to be originally native to India or Pakistan, then later introduced into Europe by the Romans. Entirely puzzling to modern botanists, however, is the fact that, although originally native to the Middle East, there is a type of Tree Onion that appears to grow wild throughout North America. Looking like a tall, slightly zany scallion, the Egyptian Walking Onion is remarkable because it is a perennial, top-setting plant, producing sets of bulblets at the tip of its stalk as well as underground. It can even produce a second clump of top-sets off the first cluster, from which the designation "Tree Onion," for this branching characteristic, derives. The "Walking" idea originated with this cultivar's unique ability to procreate by flopping over as the season ends and allowing some of the top-sets to root. In essence, the plant will literally "walk" across your garden as each generation moves out from the mother plant.

As Egyptian Walking Onions are perennial, you can start a patch once and, over the years, keep it refreshed and contained by editing or adding bulbs: if you leave a plant, it will produce a fine top-set of bulblets the next year; if you want more onions, simply plant a few new bulblets. Egyptian Walking Onion's plump, pink, shallotlike bulbs pack a power-house punch of vitamins A and C, as well as healthy doses of calcium, magnesium, and potassium, so how about slivering a bunch of these, caramelizing with a bit of extra virgin olive oil and *balsamico,* then spreading with an anchovy filet on a savory Italian crostini?

☙

❧ 26. Elberta Peach Tomato ❧
Solanum lycopersicon esculentum

According to the USDA, and despite their highly controversial culinary history, tomatoes are preferred by four out of five Americans to any other homegrown food, and over 90 percent of American home gardeners grow them.

In the annals of vegetable history, the tomato must certainly claim the crown as the edible plant with the most dramatic gastronomic turnaround. Viciously maligned, even shunned and despised by a host of cultures, including our own, well into the nineteenth century, the tomato now stands as the single most popular vegetable in current Western culture. Originally a wild, coarse, tiny-fruited thing native to Mexico and the southern Americas, most current evidence supports Central America as the first seat of domestication of this reigning popularity queen. For one thing, the Aztecs in Central America had a word for the tomato, calling it *xitomatl,* and even described it in recipes, while the writings of the ancient Peruvians, most notably the Incas, fail to include even a description of a tomato-like fruit.

Additionally, the pre-Columbian cultures of ancient Peru were fond of decorating and forming pottery and artifacts in the likenesses of their favorite food crops and, while there are many visual references to such edible plants as beans, corn, and squash, they seem to have failed to create a single identifiable image of a tomato. Tomatoes were eventually discovered, along with a host of other theretofore unknown food plants, by the marauding conquistadores from Spain and Portugal, who delivered them to the European continent in the fifteenth century.

As members of the always-suspect *Solanum* or nightshade family, tomatoes were given the original European designation of "wolf's peach" or *Lypersicon,* by the Greek physician Galen, as nightshades were

Elberta Peach Tomato

legendarily linked to werewolves. Karl Linnaeus later added the *esculen-tum,* meaning "edible," although this was an issue clearly up for debate as, although winning some culinary popularity in Spain and Italy, tomatoes were introduced into England only as questionable ornamentals. In fact, the English herbalist John Gerard, who planted them in the College of Physicians gardens in Holborne in 1590, concluded that "the whole plant" was possessed "of ranke and stinking savour."

There are literally hundreds of laudable varieties of tomatoes grown in the twentieth century, but here I recommend to you the ravishing cultivar Elberta Peach. This truly unusual tomato variety is a visual stunner and only distantly similar to the familiar round, red, run-of-the-mill type. Firstly, the Elberta Peach is immediately commendable for its uncommonly appealing foliage, which is fuzzy and of a striking grayish white coloration. These highly attractive vines are further enhanced by pretty, smallish, round- to plum-shaped fruits that are a brilliant orange-red, gaily striped longitudinally with sunny gold. The alliance of foliage as decorative as an Artemesia with fruit so vivaciously and decoratively striated is a bona fide visual triumph, perfectly suited for a vertical focal point in the garden.

Tomatoes are a fairly long-season tropical plant and insist on warm temperatures and full sun, so start in the greenhouse in 4-inch pots 4 to 6 weeks before last frost, then plant out in a well-composted, sunny spot when soil temperatures are above 60 degrees. Even though Elberta Peach is a determinate variety, do give it a stout trellis or teepee to clamber up. These beauties, which should start producing about 80 days from transplant, have a nice tangy flavor, so why not coarse-chop a few and toss with chopped fresh mint, crumbled blue cheese, and a lemony vinaigrette for a nice variation on a classic *Caprese* salad?

❧ 27. Fish Pepper ❧
Capsicum frutescens

In 1938, in an instance of what can only be described as "hot sex," a
study of the effects of capsaicin, *the heat-inducing compound in peppers,*
on the water flea (Daphnia magna) *noted a resultant "pronounced*
and continued excitatory movement of the male genital organ."

Peppers are native to the Americas alone and are actually thought to have originated in the West Indies or Jamaica, since the names of many early varieties can be traced to a Caribbean root. However, they made their way to the mainland of the southern Americas by very early on in our prehistory, Aztec remains indicating dates as early as 6500 B.C. Traveling homeward in the pockets of the gold-hungry conquistadores of the fifteenth century, hot peppers took the world by storm. Spices in general were in huge demand (thus the "spice" roads as traders plied them from Asia to northern Europe), and an alternative to the highly expensive Indian black pepper (*Piper nigrum*) was a find indeed.

Peppers made some exceedingly beneficial inroads into the realm of the more mundane challenges of life as well. For instance, one of the commonest household uses of hot peppers in cultures all over the world was and is as a burning fumigant for vermin ranging from bedbugs to rats. Ranchers in the American Southwest have been known to smear their sheep with chilies to discourage attack by wolves and, in the mid-nineteenth century, Dr. Barton of Philadelphia hailed a sprayed mixture of red pepper and tobacco as the savior of his cucumber crop from devastation by cucumber beetles.

The Fish Pepper counts both the Tabasco and the Habañero Pepper as siblings in the *Capsicum frutescens* family, although some authorities further split this group into *Capsicum frutescens* and *Capsicum chinenses.*

This captivating, pre-1870, African-American heirloom was a happy, spontaneous mutation, selected, then cultivated to add spice to the signature fare of the oyster and crab houses that grew up around the Chesapeake Bay in Maryland. Interestingly, there was a local African-American legend that held that in order for peppers to achieve their ultimate fieriness, one had to be in a "fiery" state as well. Therefore, the best Fish Peppers were said to be planted by those who were really angry. One supposes this made for all kinds of local fun.

Fish Peppers themselves are intensely visually striking as they move through an early maturation point in which the 2- to 3-inch long, pendant fruits are striped as gaily as a canopy in green and cream, then ripening to a vibrant orange with brown stripes and, finally, to a glossy, robust red. However, this pretty show is rivaled in full by the beautiful green and white variegation of the foliage of these vigorous 2-foot-tall plants. This is no run-of-the-mill margination, but a splendidly haphazard coloring in which some of the youngest leaves are virtually white while others are intricately dappled in shades of cream and emerald. All in all, a true visual virtuoso and worth a place in any vegetable garden.

As with all tropical natives, pepper plants are insistent on warm temperatures, so start them indoors about 6 weeks before the last frost in a warm, sunny window, then plant them out about a foot apart when soil is warmed up to at least 60 degrees. Culinarily, in deference to their illustrious Chesapeake Bay heritage, why not consider adding some spice to your life and a few of these to a big pot of crab gumbo? I'll leave that recipe to you.

Fish Pepper

28. 'German Red Strawberry' Tomato
Solanum lycopersicon esculentum

In a marvelous example of the stunning single-mindedness of the French, when the tomato or "Moors Apple" (pomei di moro), so named because it had been carried from Spain into Italy by the Moors, was introduced into France, the French immediately mistook the name to be "pomo d'amour," and so the popular designation of the tomato as "love apple" was born.

The first domesticated tomatoes were cultivated by the Mayan and Aztec cultures of Central and South America, and were thought to have been introduced into cookery by the Mayans. As descendants of the wild *cerasiformes,* the earliest domestic varieties were undoubtedly small-fruited as well, and these were the specimens that first made the voyage to Spain and Portugal with the returning conquistadores in the fifteenth century. The European response to these exotic new cultivars was decidedly mixed, many cultures associating the tomato with poisonous members of the *Solanacea* family, chiefly mandrake and deadly nightshade, and the English, in particular, believing tomatoes to be highly suspect and growing them only as a curiosity.

Deadly Nightshade (*Atropus belladonna*), the *Solanacea* that probably bears the closest resemblance to the tomato, is a poisonous plant employed for centuries in Europe as a combination hallucinogenic and cosmetic. The hallucinogenic properties of the plant included visions and the sensation of flying or floating, which undoubtedly led to nightshade's close association with witchcraft. Old German folklore also maintained that witches, in a practice known as "lycanthropy," utilized *Atropus belladonna* to evoke werewolves. Thus the common Old German name for tomatoes, which translated to "wolf peach," was one that followed the tomato around the continent for centuries.

The ancient cosmetic employment of nightshade is equally interesting, its botanical name *belladonna* translating literally to "beautiful woman" in direct reference to this practice. As fashions come and go, it was evidently desirable among medieval ladies to sport a wide-eyed gaze and, in order to impart this "limpid pool" aspect, they were given to dilating their pupils by applying a few drops of nightshade extract. One of the few medicinal references to the tomato itself occurs, strangely, in the English herbalist William Salmon's *Botanologia* of 1710, in which he recommends the tomato for repressing "vapors in women" and "fits of mother," as well as for headache, gout, and sciatica.

Let me now recommend here the lovely 'German Red Strawberry' tomato, an antique German heirloom, as neither an hallucinogen, a cosmetic, or a cure, but as one of the most unusually beautiful tomatoes around. For starts, this gorgeous, deep blood-orange "ox-heart" type tomato is shaped exactly like an immense strawberry, with fruit ranging anywhere from 8 ounces to 1 pound. As well, its coloration is not just your run-of-the-mill "tomato" orange, but is as richly intense and dramatic as oriental lacquer, both inside and out. An excellent producer, particularly for an ox-heart, these really uniquely lovely fruits are borne on vigorous, indeterminate vines.

Being Central and South American natives, all tomatoes like it sunny and hot, so start the pretty 'German Red Strawberry' indoors 4 to 6 weeks before the last frost, then plant out when soil temperatures have reached at least 60 degrees in well-composted soil and full sun. Mulch well and water deeply throughout the season and you should be harvesting these fair fruits in about 80 days from transplant. The flavor of the 'German Red Strawberry' is exceptionally full-bodied and sweet with just the right amount of acid, so I suggest coarsely chopping these with garlic, basil, salt, pepper, and olive oil, then tossing with fresh, drained pasta for a sublime summer supper.

'German Red Strawberry' Tomato

🎐 29. Giant Chinese Red Mustard 🎐
Brassica uncea Chinensis

In the decidedly wishfully inclined African nation of Tanganyika, sun-dried mustard leaves and flowers are popularly smoked so that erstwhile thrill seekers can "get in touch with the spirits."

Identifying a Chinese Mustard is a bit like stepping into a botanical minefield: a new, bewildering variation exploding up at every step. The exact botanical refinements that separate a Chinese cabbage from a Chinese mustard and a whole host of other related *Brassicas,* are suspiciously obscure and, in fact, the current botanical and common divisions, *Brassica rapa* being the Chinese cabbage and *Brassica uncea* var. *Chinensis* being the Chinese mustard, are really late Western attempts to define and conquer. The truth is, both families bear offspring not only possessed of leaf shapes ranging from the neatly spoonlike to winged, unwinged, notched, feathered, and curled, but also running the gamut from the compact and cabbage-like to the monstrously loose and clumpy, and, on the "bite" scale, from becomingly mild to blisteringly sharp.

The ancestors of these varied *Brassicas* have grown wild in the Far East probably since the dawn of vegetation, although their first literary mention in China does not occur until the fifth century B.C. Oddly, unlike the ubiquitous Indian mustard, the family of Chinese mustards and cabbages has never been widely received outside the Orient, Chinese writers reporting in the fifteenth century that, while Chinese cabbages and mustards could be obtained in Malaysia and the East Indies, they were not commonly grown even there. During the eighteenth century, European missionaries sent seeds of several varieties back home to Europe, but again these seemed to have failed to win favor on the Continent. In reality, it hasn't been until the twentieth century and the true globalization of both culture and cuisine that these beautiful and delicious Asian cole crops have met with justifiably wide acceptance.

The Giant Chinese Red Mustard is mustard anyone familiar with mustard greens would identify as one, if only for its peppery bite. However, let me also report that, for sheer beauty of form and coloration, this is one of the two or three plants I grow that is most remarked upon by visitors to the garden, whether they have any idea of its exact identity or not. To catch a ray of late afternoon sun illuminating a stand of these brilliant, peridot green-ribbed, plumelike leaves, each edged with a rich ruby ruffle, the whole extravagant crown growing to a stately 18 inches tall and 14 inches around, is a dazzling sight indeed. You'll also be happy to learn that, historically and across many cultures, mustards have been employed as remedies for everything from arthritis, lumbago, rheumatism, and stomach and bladder disorders, to tumors, abscesses, skin eruptions, and ulcers, and that a scant cupful will provide you with 60 percent of your recommended daily vitamin A, all of your vitamin C, and about one fifth of your iron.

Additionally, Giant Chinese Red Mustard is quite winter-hardy and slow to bolt, and seems to remain blissfully unscathed by insects or disease, so direct sow in early spring and again in midsummer for fall harvesting, planting ½ inch deep and thinning to about 18 inches apart. The bright tasting, crimson-tinged succulence of the young leaves in a salad is a gustatory delight, and the older, spicier leaves are wonderful used as a potherb in soups or stews. I recommend coarsely chopping some of the more mature leaves of this regal, ruby-toned cultivar and braising with a bit of garlic and diced salt pork as a wonderful accompaniment to a ham or lamb roast.

GIANT CHINESE RED MUSTARD

❧ 30. Giant Red Celery ❧
Apium graveolens

*"Sellery . . . for its high and grateful Taste, is ever plac'd in the middle of
the Grande Sallet at our Great Men's Tables and Praetor's Feasts as the
Grace of the whole Board."*

— John Evelyn, *Acetaria: A Discourse of Sallets*, 1699

Our modern-day celery is a descendant of "wild celery," also
called "meadow parsley" or "smallage," a plant native to the
Mediterranean basin and cultivated as an herbal flavoring by
many civilizations for thousands of years. In fact, the classical funerary
plant so often portrayed in Egyptian tomb paintings and long believed to
be parsley, is believed by many to actually be the original, wild form of
celery, which can still be found growing wild in marshy locales all over
Europe, the Caucasus, and Asia Minor, having been mentioned in China
as early as the fifth century A.D. The oldest record of the word *celery* is a
ninth-century poem of obscure French or Italian origin in which the
plant's medicinal merits were positively articulated, including popular
employment as a laxative, diuretic, cure for jaundice, and poultice for
the bites of "wild beastes."

Apium graveolens, the more refined descendant of the original, ancient
cultivar, was first developed as a medicinal herb in Italy in the sixteenth
century, first used as a kitchen herb in France in 1623 and, by the middle
of the seventeenth century, the stalks and leaves were being commonly
consumed in both countries, usually with a dressing of oil and vinegar.
By the mid-eighteenth century, Swedish families of means were enjoying
the winter luxury of blanched celery stalks stored in root cellars, and
celery had found its way to the New World, four varieties reported under
cultivation in Europe's North American colonies by 1806. In the twentieth century, Dutch farmers settling around Kalamazoo, Michigan and

putting their knowledge of Dutch "muck" soil (soil containing a disproportionate amount of decomposed vegetable matter) to admirable use, spawned America's current multimillion dollar celery industry.

The celery variety Giant Red is a justifiably vivid presence in the garden, being possessed of an attractive, more open growing habit than most other celeries, the stalks rising to a robust 10 to 13 inches. Additionally, Giant Red is as remarkable for its signature coloration as it is for its outstanding architectural form. Red celeries are not an especially new development, ten, mainly English, including the Giant Red, being listed in Vilmorin-Andrieux's *The Vegetable Garden* in 1885, bearing such decorative names as "Incomparable Crimson," "Laing's Mammoth," and "Sulham's Prize Pink." Most of these are not the true red of, say, a rhubarb chard stem, but are more a green flushed with a bronzy, burgundy red: a very attractive color for a tall crown of classically ribbed stalks tufted with feathery, red-blushed greenery. A patch of these stately plants makes a particularly pleasing anchor for a vegetable bed, offset with the blue of a *Brassica* or the light green of a Butterhead Lettuce.

Celery does best when started indoors and planted out at about 3 inches high, when soil is warmed to above 60 degrees. Therefore, start in seed cups 6 weeks before your frost date and plant out about the first of June, spacing plants a good 14 to 16 inches apart. Fertilize well as celery is a particularly heavy feeder. Giant Red has a vigorous, distinctive celery flavor that makes it perfect for standing up to soups or stews, so why not add a confetti of this striking cultivar to some summery gazpacho or a hearty fall stew?

GIANT RED CELERY

GOLDEN SWEET EDIBLE-PODDED PEA

❧ 31. Golden Sweet Edible-Podded Pea ❧
Pisum sativum

"The chapter of the pea endures always; the impatience to consume them, the pleasure of watching them be consumed, and the joy of consuming them again are the three points our princes have debated for four days. . . . It is a fashion and a furor."

—Madame de Maintenon, May 16, 1696

The origin of the wild pea is somewhat obscure for being so early, but Ethiopia, the Mediterranean, and central Asia are usually mentioned. Charred pea remains have been recovered in Turkey dating from 7500 to 7000 B.C., found in Egyptian tombs of the Twelfth Dynasty, and, biblically, were among the foods brought to David in the desert (II Sam. 17:28). They were the principal British food crop even before the Norman conquests, and were finally delivered to the New World by Christopher Columbus in 1493. They were soon everywhere you wanted to be.

"Fresh" or "green" peas, versus dried, were not eaten until the seventeenth century, when the first fresh variety was perfected in Holland. They created such a rage at the court of Louis IV in France that they sold for fifty crowns a pint and caused Madame de Maintenon to additionally opine: "There are women who, after dining, and dining well, demand peas before sleeping at the risk of indigestion." Thomas Knight of the British Horticultural Society began experimenting with hybridization in 1787, producing pea cultivars increasingly pleasing to the palette, which, judging from the French reaction, may have been playing with fire. This toying with the pea continued in the nineteenth century in the work of the Moravian monk Gregor Mendel, father of genetics, who founded that science by demonstrating that, through hybridization, the pea's dominant and recessive genes could be identified by a fixed ratio.

The Edible-Podded Pea is yet a further refinement of the common pea of old, closely resembling it in most characteristics save that the pods are flatter, more tender, and the entire pod, including the immature seeds, is edible. The Golden Sweet Edible-Podded Pea, a Far East Indian heirloom, was first collected at a market in Delhi in the 1990s by Kent Whealy of The Seed Savers Exchange. It's the only yellow-colored, edible-podded pea in their entire collection of over 1,000 varieties and, as far as I know, is totally unique. The pods are a show-stopping, bright lemon yellow, and there's not another sugar snap or snow pea that can begin to rival them for sheer visual extravagance. And, as if that wasn't enough, these viners, prettily growing to 6 feet up a trellis or teepee, will reward you with a plethora of beautiful, two-toned purple flowers to boot.

The Golden Sweet Edible-Podded Pea is a cool-season vegetable, as are all peas. However, being an East Indian (tropical) and edible-podded variety, it displays a wider adaptive and higher temperature tolerance than do others. Plant out around a trellis or other support system 1 inch deep and 3 or 4 inches apart in early spring and you should be enjoying these sunshiny beauties in 60 to 70 days. The pods are crisply tender when picked small (more mature pods will require stringing before cooking) and, of course, are excellent simply steamed or in a stir-fry. However, in honor of this one's Far East Indian origins, how about serving it as an hors d'oeuvre by batter-frying with a dash of cumin, curry, and coriander, then dipping in a sweet vinegar and mint sauce? The seeds, tan with purple flecks, can also be dried and added to soups.

❦ 32. Green Zebra Tomato ❦
Solanum lycopersicon esculentum

In 1887 in Nix v. Hedden, *in order to protect the American farmer from untaxed imports, Justice Gray of the U.S. Supreme Court ruled that the tomato, although botanically speaking a fruit, was for official purposes a vegetable, citing: "tomatoes are the fruit of a vine, just as are cucumbers, squashes, beans and peas. But in the common language of the people . . . all these are vegetables, which are grown in kitchen gardens, and . . . are usually served at dinner in, with, or after the soup, fish or meats . . . and not, like fruits generally, as dessert."*

The top tomato-producing countries in the world are the United States, China, Turkey, Italy, and India, with the United States topping the list, Americans consuming over 12 million tons of tomatoes annually, which is a lot of salsa. Culinary stardom, however, came very late in time for the much-maligned tomato. Prized historically by the natives of South America and Mexico, tomatoes found their way into Spain and Portugal near the turn of the sixteenth century with the returning conquistadores, but there they languished for centuries in a kind of gastronomic purgatory. In fact, it really wasn't until the second half of the nineteenth century that tomatoes finally achieved the kind of universal acceptance they currently enjoy.

For instance, the first cookbook to mention tomatoes on the European continent was published in Naples in 1692, but it wasn't until 1752 that English cooks took the gastronomic leap, although with remarkable trepidation, when they began employing the tomato in the flavoring of soups. The distain with which the tomato was first greeted in North America is a thing of legend, although, finally, by 1865, horticulturist Fearing Burr was listing 24 varieties in his *The Field and Garden Vegetables of America*, writing: ". . . to a majority of tastes, the tomato's

GREEN ZEBRA TOMATO

flavor is not at first particularly agreeable; but by those accustomed to its use, it is esteemed one of the best, as it is also reputed to be one of the most healthful, of all garden vegetables."

Out of the bevy of beautiful tomato varieties available to us today, I believe the best I can do in this volume is to offer up to the reader a brief, becoming range in terms of form, color, and taste and, certainly, even an abbreviated list would not be complete without the exotic Green Zebra. This beautiful twentieth-century hybrid was developed by Tom Wagner of Tater Mater Seeds in 1985 and, as you might assume, it is both green and striated. When ripe, Green Zebra's lovely 3-ounce fruits are striped from stem to base in complex shadings of yellow, amber, and deep green, and borne on handsome, indeterminate vines growing to 8 feet or more. I'm very fond of growing Green Zebra up a teepee with a medium-yellow or red fruited variety like Garden Peach or Enchantment for nice color contrast.

Transplant 4- to 6-week-old Green Zebra seedlings out into the garden in a well-mulched, sunny spot 2 weeks after your frost date and you should be harvesting these sweet, zingy beauties about 77 days from transplant. Considered a uniquely delicious salad tomato, Green Zebra's light green flesh is exceptionally flavorful, with a nice balance of the sweet and the tart. As well, all tomatoes are excellent sources of vitamins A and C, lycopene, magnesium, and iron, so I suggest chopping up a basketful of these with some Vidalia Onion, a jalapeño pepper, fresh cilantro, a shake of salt, and a squeeze of lime juice into a gorgeous green salsa.

33. Habañero Pepper
Capsicum frutescens

"There once was a young girl from France,

Who kept this hot fruit in her pants.

She just had one pepper,

But became a high stepper,

And invented the Mexican Hat Dance!"

— Gary L. Simmons, *Gary's House of Whacks*

(Chili Pepper website)

What makes a hot pepper so "hot"? It involves a complex of compounds called capsaicinoids, which, contrary to the popular belief that the seeds of the pepper carry the biggest "bite," actually develop most prominently (and warmly) in the fleshy, interior cross-ribs of the fruit. The seeds are hot only by proximity. If, when the pepper is cut open, these ribs are possessed of a light orangey color (versus a darker one matching the exterior of the pepper), the pepper is sure to be a potent one. Additionally, many people are mistaken in the belief that hot peppers are irritants to the digestive system. In fact, members of the *Capsicum* family have quite the opposite effect, being both beneficial to digestion and actually soothing to the stomach. It's also interesting to note that, in terms of health benefits, a hot pepper can contain as much as six times the amount of vitamin C as in an orange, the highest level being found in the immature green fruit.

In 1912, American pharmacist Wilbur L. Scoville developed a method of measuring the "heat" in a hot pepper, or scoring capsaicinoid content, which is still employed today. Measured in "Scoville Units," sweet bell peppers, for instance, clock in at 0 because they contain no capsaicinoids at all, while jalapeños score from 2,500 to 4,000 on the Scoville scale. Tabascos and Cayennes step into the ring at 60,000 to 80,000 units, but the fiery crown goes to the pulchritudinous Habañero Pepper, which registers a tongue-tingling 200,000 to 300,000 Scoville Units on average. The Red Savina Habañero, claiming the *Guinness Book of Records* prize as the world's hottest spice, rates an astonishing 580,000 Scoville Units. Do not try this one at home.

Considered by many aficionados to have the loveliest fruit as well as the hottest bite of any chili, the Habañero Pepper is technically the species *Capsicum Chinense Jacquin.* The name "Habañero" connotes "from Havana" and the popular belief is that the peppers made their way to the Yucatan Peninsula, where 1,500 tons of Habañeros are harvested each year, from Cuba. These exceedingly pretty fruits, cousins to the tinier Scotch Bonnet Pepper, are also thought to resemble a Scottish "tam" in shape, although I've habitually noted their visual kinship to tiny Oriental or Turkish-inspired lanterns, ranging in size from 1½ to 3 inches. In spring, they start a nice, nascent green, then ripen through a blushingly peachy stage to assume the beautiful, deep, lacquery orange coloration that is their ultimate achievement. The bushy plants grow to about 24 inches and the light green, serrated leaves are very attractive as well.

Plant Habañero seeds in 4-inch pots 6 weeks before last frost, keep the soil warm, and watch for germination in about 18 to 25 days. Once seedlings start to appear, move the pots to your sunniest windowsill, then transplant out when nighttime temperatures are consistently above 60 degrees. Green, unripe fruit will generally be produced in 55 to 75 days after setting out and ripe fruit in about 100 days. I would suggest drying your Habañeros and storing the powder for future use, as a pinch will go an extremely long way. Do wear gloves when handling them and, for goodness sake, don't touch your eyes!

HABAÑERO PEPPER

❧ 34. Hillbilly Tomato ❧
Solanum lypersicon esculentum

*The fabled "golden apples" of Greek legend, given to Hera at her wed-
ding to Zeus as tokens of eternal life and fertility, then guarded by the
willowy Hesperides until they were spirited away by Hercules, were, in
fact, one of the earliest forms of the "pomo d'oro" or tomato.*

T he tomato originated spontaneously in the coastal highlands of
western South America and small, scruffy wild tomatoes can
still be found growing in the seaside mountains of Peru, Chile,
and Ecuador. The wild tomato was a simple, tiny, two-celled creature
until a friendly genetic mutation occurred, resulting in the large, ruffled
and lobed, multicelled fruit with which we are all now so familiar. The
tomato was domesticated by the Mayans and Aztecs and, at the end of
the fifteenth century, was carried into the Mediterranean basin of
Europe by the returning conquistadores. In 1544, Pietro Andrae
Matthioli, the Italian herbalist, classified the suspicious new import as
one of the mandrake family, which were close cousins to deadly nightshade, which is exactly when the centuries of suspicion and misinfor-
mation surrounding the tomato began to pick up steam.

Matthioli was also the first botanist to refer to the tomato as the *mala
aurea,* or "bad golden thing," supporting the theory that the first tomatoes
introduced into Europe were yellow, which he then transmuted into
pomo d'oro or "golden apple." He describes them as "flattened like a
Melrose (a type of apple) and segmented, green at first and when ripe, of
a golden color" and wrote that they were "eaten in Italy with oil, salt and
pepper." It wasn't until 1590 that tomatoes made their way into England,
although John Parkinson, apothecary to James I, proclaimed that, while
they were eaten by people in hot countries to "coole and quench the
heate and thirst of hot stomaches," British gardeners grew them only as
a curiosity and for their titillatingly suspicious reputation. By the end of

the sixteenth century, the Dutch botanist Rembert Dodoens had observed: "two sortes, one red and the other yellow, but in all other poyntes they be lyke."

The magnificent Hillbilly Tomato is a gorgeous heirloom that marries the glories of both varieties, boasting both golden and ruby-hued flesh. Hillbilly, its name true to its roots, is a turn-of-the-century, North American variety first cultivated in the Smokey Mountains of West Virginia. The enormous, pleasingly asymmetrical and old-fashioned, bicolored fruit is a deep orange-red, marbled and streaked with brilliant gold, and cutting into one of these voluptuous, 1- to 2- pound beauties to reveal the strikingly marbled interior is one of those moments of true culinary revelation. The stout vines are indeterminate and the leaves are notably and interestingly of the "potato leaf" type. In a family in which foliage is generally fairly run-of-the-mill, this is a substantial bonus as well.

As with most larger-fruited cultivars, Hillbilly will need a good 3 months of warm, sunny cultivation in a richly composted soil with some hefty trellising provided for them to climb. Therefore, start in seed cups 4 weeks before your last frost date, then transplant out around your trellis 2 weeks after it, when soil is well warmed up. Also, in general, tomatoes have deep root systems, so do water adequately through the season. Hillbilly's big, meaty fruit are wonderfully sweet and fruity in flavor, and their size makes them perfect for sandwiches, so I recommend a thick wedge between 2 slices of thin white bread slicked with mayonnaise and topped with a grinding of fresh pepper. Absolute ambrosia.

HILLBILLY TOMATO

IMPERIAL STAR ARTICHOKE

❧ 35. Imperial Star Artichoke ❧
Cynara scolymus

In 1947 in Castroville, California, a startlingly young Norma Jean Baker, soon to be known to the world as Marilyn Monroe, got her first leg up in life when the "artichoke capital of the world" elected her its very first Artichoke Festival Queen.

The artichoke was first cultivated as a crop in the first century A.D. in the region around Naples in Italy. This majestic but unlikely looking edible was further popularized by the famously intrigue-ridden Catherine de Medici, who, when not dabbling in murder, mayhem, and political manipulation, was known to adore them. When she was married in 1533, at the age of fourteen, to Henry II of France, she brought the artichoke, along with her native cunning, with her as part of her dowry. Henry apparently took the tasty bait and earned himself a reputation as a celebrated artichoke glutton in an era in which artichokes were considered to be a powerful aphrodisiac. It is unclear to this writer whether this was an element of the scheming Catherine's plan.

Artichokes were grown at Monticello by Thomas Jefferson as early as 1770, although, unlike in European cultivation, they were and still are not hardy on the northeastern seaboard and have be treated as annuals. Jefferson conceded this small drawback in a letter to a Madame de Tessé of Paris in 1805 when he wrote: "We can have neither figs nor artichokes without protection from the winter." By the mid-nineteenth century, however, French immigrants had brought artichoke plants to Louisiana where the first perennial Creole artichokes were grown. Then, in the late nineteenth century, Italian immigrants commenced their planting of the first of California's fabled commercial artichoke fields in the area south of San Francisco, where acres of artichokes now surround the "Artichoke Capital of the World": the tiny and eccentric hamlet of Castroville, California.

The artichoke's nearest relatives are the cardoon and the sunflower, and it is one of the true glories of the garden. The most refined of thistles, these large, neatly carved, almost prehistoric-looking buds grow to magnificent proportions on sturdy 4- to 5-foot stems amid gorgeously architectural, deeply cut, silver-green leaves that arch fountainlike from the crown. In fact, artichokes are so visually splendid that one often sees them planted in purely decorative flower borders. I recommend here the green Imperial Star Artichoke, first developed in 1991 by Wayne Schrader and Keith Mayberry of the California Cooperative Extension Service, over the "Green Globe" common to the California artichoke industry, as Imperial Star was bred specifically for the shorter, annual season of our more northerly climes. This is very good news for us northern gardeners who, until that moment, had no recourse without the employment of extensive greenhouse space.

To grow Imperial Star as an annual, sow seeds in 6-inch pots indoors during late winter and transplant the handsome seedlings into the garden after frost, spacing 3 or 4 feet apart. Like all artichokes, Imperial Stars prefer rich, well-prepared soil, plenty of sun, and even moisture. Mulch plants well to keep roots cool and moist in summer. It is the edible, undeveloped flower buds of the artichoke one consumes, though one is sorely tempted to leave them uncut in order to watch the stately, purple, thistlelike flowers develop. However, if you must harvest, simplicity is of the essence: cut off the head sharply below the lowest leaves, snip off the thorny tips, steam till cooked, then serve hot with melted butter or cold with a nice, tarragon-scented mayonnaise.

36. Jarrahdale Pumpkin
Cucurbita pepo

For sixty years, from 1778 to 1848, David Wilbur of Westerly, Rhode Island, known forever after as "the New England pumpkin-scratcher," took to the woods and remained there, shunning humanity and living off the land, his only human contact being the strange hieroglyphs and signs he scratched onto his neighbor's field pumpkins.

As a member of the *Cucurbitae* family, along with squash, melons, and cucumbers, all characterized by their signature Curbit hard shell and vining habit, the pumpkin constitutes another of the world's oldest food crops, seeds having been found in Mexico dating to 8000 B.C. Unlike melons and cucumbers, which are of Far East Indian ancestry, pumpkins and squash are originally native only to the Americas. In 1493, it was Christopher Columbus himself who delivered the very first pumpkin seeds to the European continent, but the resulting early crops were, oddly, only thought fit for animal fodder. The German herbalist Leonard Fuchs describes this exotic and highly colored new-comer in his *New Herball* in 1543, calling it the "Ocean Cucumber."

There has been age-old debate among botanists as to what constitutes a pumpkin versus a melon versus a squash and, really, this is a massive gray area. All, in fact, shared the same Latin root *pepo* either in their common or botanical designations (there have been later delineations), *pepo* deriving from the Greek *pepon,* meaning "cooked by the sun," which was later manhandled by the early French into *poupon,* which was then transmuted by the English to *pompion,* and then further bastardized by the American colonists into our current "pumpkin," the diminutive "kin" being added for sheer sauciness, one imagines.

Long before the advent of the European colonists, however, Native Americans were fantastic pumpkin eaters and, from about 2000 B.C.

JARRAHDALE PUMPKIN

onwards, they found countless ways to employ the sweet, long-keeping meat of this prolific native cultivar. Aside from enjoying pumpkin baked, boiled, roasted, fried, parched, and dried, they also ground dried pumpkin bits into flour for baking, consumed the seeds as possibly the world's first health-food snack, and even dried strips of pumpkin flesh to weave into mats.

The Jarrahdale or Australian Pumpkin is one of the most stunning vegetables (actually a fruit) that I can suggest. Its form is a classic, true pumpkin shape: uniformly and deeply ribbed and rather rounder than it is tall, with a slight indentation at the top. However, it is its exterior texture that is really remarkable, resembling nothing so much as the finest Chinese celadon porcelain. The skin is richly polishd and of the most divinely subtle and somehow "deep" gray-green hue. This amazingly decorative Australian heirloom also boasts a fantastic interior surprise, as its flesh, far from being the general issue orange, is a brilliantly clear, true yellow. The size of the fruits can vary anywhere from 13 to 15 inches in diameter, and this variety is also a long-keeper, so you can enjoy its pure physicality in a bowl or on a tabletop for a bit before you dine on it.

The Jarrahdale Pumpkin has a fairly long season at around 90 days, so direct sow 3 or 4 seeds of this beautiful heirloom in well-mulched and composted hills at least 6 feet apart as soon as is possible after danger of frost. Thin to the strongest 2 plants per 6 to 8 square feet, mulch well, water frequently, and feed with a liquid fertilizer at least twice during the season. The flesh of the almost unearthly Jarrahdale is legendarily light and smooth and would be perfect for a warming, ginger-scented, unexpectedly cadmium-tinted winter pudding or custard.

❧ 37. Kale Nero di Toscana ❧
Brassica oleracea acephala

'Jersey Kale,' a long-lived heirloom variety described in Vilmorin's The Vegetable Garden *of 1885, apparently reached such imposing heights (to 9 feet tall), that, after the flowering tip was snapped off, their woody stems were traditionally fashioned into popular and exceedingly well-priced walking sticks.*

Brassicas are a rather marvelous example of the natural law that holds that remarkable, even visionary discoveries can be made by simple, long-term, rudderless refinement by people focused, merely and securely, on their own personal whims. And these very individual visions can be as myriad as the human race, which is why we count kale, cabbage, kohlrabi, cauliflower, broccoli, Brussels sprouts, and all cress and mustards as members of the *Brassica oleracea* family, a descendant from what was probably a single, wild mustard of Mediterranean extraction. The only differences between these plants are those introduced over the history of their selection by this or that specific native preference. By the fifth century B.C., however, a widespread predilection for ever larger-leaved varieties led, from pretty much one end of Europe to the other, to the development of the vegetable we now know as kale.

Kale was also most probably the item referred to in medieval times as the ubiquitous "colewort," a catchall kind of *Brassica* moniker listed in every early *Herball*, including both Gerard and Evelyn, experts feeling that, from visual evidence in such paintings as Brueghel's "The Numbering at Bethlehem," the colewort's closest contemporary progeny are the non-curly kales. At Bayleaf Garden in England, they've chosen the American collard and the 'Hungry Gap' Kale to employ in their restoration as closest to the plants that were described by Jon Gardener in the fourteenth century. In general, however, kales seem to suffer from a kind a dull stalwartness of reputation, gardeners appreciating them more for their willingness to grow where others won't and withstand brutal frost with not only a smile, but with increased sweetness, rather than for their aesthetic or culinary merits.

One of the most ornamental kales in existence is the variety called 'Nero di Toscana,' alternately known as 'Lacinato,' 'Dinosaur,' or 'Black Palm Tree' Kale, an Italian heirloom dating to the eighteenth century. This dramatic cultivar makes a perfectly stunning and totally unique color statement in the garden: a wonderful, dark punctuation point boasting dark blue-green to almost black, heavily blistered leaves, rumpled and puckered like a huge Savoy, each leaf 2 to 4 inches across and often more than a foot long, curled under along the entire margin, the entire plant growing to 2 feet tall. And, in contrast to its striking appearance, the flavor of this truly ornamental edible is famously sweet and mild, especially after a nip of frost. And if that's not enough, it's also as nutritious as it is visually arresting, being absolutely chockablock with vitamin C and folic acid.

Kale is a fairly long-season plant and you want to time its maturation with the advent of hard fall, as flavor is always infinitely better after a couple of real frosts. So count back about 80 days from the start of your frostiest (or merely coolest) season, and plant then: for instance, around mid-July where we are. Space plants 14 inches apart in all directions in fertile soil with a neutral pH, and a good supply of calcium. Leaves are best eaten when small and tender, before too much fiber develops. Try this imposing brute sautéed with a smashed clove of garlic in a splash of olive oil, then braised in chicken stock until wilted and, finally, sprinkled with fresh *parmesano*.

KALE NERO DI TOSCANA

❦ 38. Leek 'Blue Solaise' ❦

Allium porrum

"I like the leeke above all herbes and flowers.

When first we wore the same the field was ours.

The Leeke is white and greene, wherby is ment

That Britaines are both stout and eminent;

Next to the Lion and the Unicorn,

The Leeke the fairest emblyn that is worne."

— B. I. Harleian, *A Collection of Pedigrees,*

fifteenth-century manuscript

Leeks, as members of the ancient *Allium* family, were probably being consumed by our prehistoric ancestors long before the advent of farming or even written language. Most botanists agree that *Alliums,* actually members of the greater *Liliacceae* or lily family, have been under domestic cultivation for at least 5,000 years and, being storable, transportable, and easily grown in a broad spectrum of soils and climates, probably constitute one of the world's earliest food crops. In Numbers 11:5 of the Bible, the leek and its cousins the onion and garlic are among the food plants pined for by the children of Israel following their great exodus: "We remember the fish, which we did eat in Egypt freely, the cucumbers and the melons and the leeks and the onions and the garlic." Thought to be central Asian in origin, leeks were often portrayed in Egyptian tomb paintings, and one petrified leek was even unearthed clasped in the hand of a royal mummy.

In India, however and interestingly, an ordinance of the sixth century B.C. proclaimed that leeks were prohibited from being consumed by the "twice born," and were fit only for the lower orders. In the first century A.D., Nero ate leeks to clear his voice for singing and, for this hopeful habit, he was derisively called *Porrophagus* or "leek-eater," and, in that same century, the Romans introduced leeks into England and Wales. By the twelfth century, the leek had become the Welsh national symbol, worn in one's hat on St. David's Day in remembrance of St. David, who, in the sixth century, induced the Britons to wear leeks on their helmets to distinguish them from the Saxons in battle. Additionally, leeks were valued for their herbal benefits, an Old English adage cautioning one to: "Eat leeks in Lide [March] and ramsins [wild garlic] in May and all the years after physicians may play."

The strappingly handsome 'Blue Solaise' Leek is a French heirloom and one of the great visual punctuators of the vegetable garden. The very large, thick shafts of these beauties are topped with an architectural cockade of elegantly arching, truly blue leaves that will turn violet in the fall. For a "true blue" note in the garden, particularly juxtaposed with some burgundy and acid green foliage, there is nothing to beat the 'Blue Solaise.' As well, these stately columns of edible vegetation are extremely sweet and also cold resistant, so they're excellent for short seasons and even winter harvest, as I've been known to pull these garden stalwarts out of the snow in March.

Leeks are also exceptionally carefree in the garden as, like other members of the *Allium* family, they seem to come with their own built-in pest resistance. They do, however, have quite a long growing season, usually 100 to 120 days, so start them in a seed tray indoors 6 to 8 weeks before last frost, then plant out in early spring. Leeks like moisture and can also tolerate some shade, so feel free to plant them in one of your less sunny corners of the garden. Employ these in a cool summer vichyssoise or a warming, winter leek-and-potato potage.

ॐ

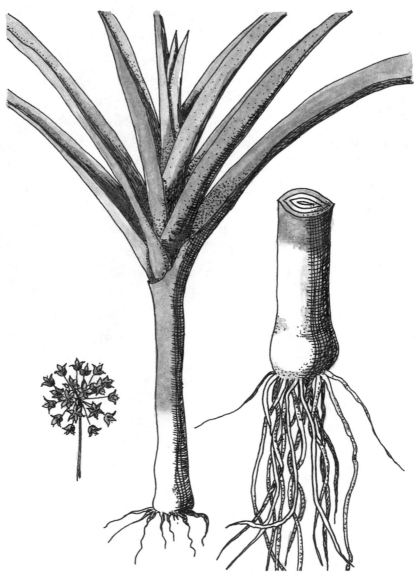

LEEK 'BLUE SOLAISE'

LEMON DROP PEPPER

❦ 39. Lemon Drop Pepper ❦
Capsicum frutescens

In 1983, NYC transit officials, in an apparent bid to add a bit of spice to daily urban travel, took to dusting subway tokens with pepper powder so that unscrupulous teenagers would stop trying to suck them out of the turnstiles.

Peppers have had an incredibly long history in the early lore of the Americas, excavations at such sites as Machu Pichu and Tenochtitlan having revealed myriad ceremonial emblems and culinary and artisan utensils formed into likenesses of the pepper dating as far back as 5200 B.C. Called "uchu" by the Incas, peppers were so highly valued by that astounding civilization that, in a show of fortitude as a boy grew into manhood, he was required to give them up. Additionally, because of the homage paid this genus, "Uchu" was the name given to the first Peruvian king, who, according to legend, sprang godlike with his seven brothers and sisters from a cleft in a rock near Cuzco, Peru.

From the Americas, hot peppers were dispersed by the earliest explorers to the Iberian Peninsula of Spain, then onto the Mediterranean and Europe. They were being cultivated in both India and Africa by the sixteenth century, with three varieties growing in India by 1542. From there, they moved on to Turkey, where they came to be known as "Turkish Peppers" to differentiate them from the highly valued but unrelated black pepper. They eventually made their way into Hungary in the late sixteenth century with Emperor Suleiman the Magnificent, becoming the foundation of the famous Hungarian paprika industry. For many years, Szeged, Hungary, was the home of the world's greatest pepper market.

Oddly, although a South and Central American native, hot peppers were only introduced to North America in the seventeenth century by the earliest European settlers, who carried them back across the ocean from Portugal and Spain. The tardy pepper, however, was ultimately warmly greeted in North America, and a cousin of the Lemon Drop, the Jalapeño Pepper, was honored by being made the first *Capsicum* in space, when it was brought aboard the space shuttle *Columbia* by astronaut Bill Lenoir in 1982.

The Lemon Drop Pepper is every bit as winsome as its name, though don't mistake this one for anything remotely sweet: it may be small, but it packs an extremely hot punch. Historically an ancient Peruvian seasoning pepper, these bright yellow, conical-shaped beauties are so prolifically borne, they decorate their plant as festively as a sunny string of Christmas lights. Plants 2 feet high and equally wide are covered with dozens of fruits ranging to about 2 or 3 inches long, with the added adornment of lovely, tiny white flowers spotted in chartreuse. This is surely another pepper to recommend for pot culture, as a plant of Lemon Drop Pepper will brighten any spot on your terrace immeasurably.

Start Lemon Drop seeds indoors, 6 weeks before your last frost in 4-inch pots, sown ½ inch deep. The best germination rates occur when the soil temperature is between 72 to 80 degrees. Look for germination in about 10 to 15 days and then, once the soil temperature is well warmed up, transplant out into a sunny location, working a good amount of compost into the soil before planting. These lemony lookers have an intensely hot, citrusy flavor, so how about making up a big bottle of vinegar with a few of these and some bruised stalks of lemon grass? Let steep in a sunny window for a few weeks, then enjoy a splash with a favorite fish or game recipe.

॰

❧ 40. Lettuce 'Forellenschluss' ❧
Lactuca sativa

"No marvel then that they were by the Ancients called "sana," by way
of eminency, and so highly valu'd by the great (Caesar) Augustus that,
attributing his Recovery of a dangerous Sickness to them, 'tis reported,
he erected a Statue and built an Altar to this noble Plant."

— John Evelyn, *Acetaria: A Discourse of Sallets,* 1699

Historically, lettuces of the ancient world were divided into two main camps: the cabbage-headed lettuces, which were of a round, relatively loose-leaved habit, and the "Cos" or "Romaine" lettuces, of a tighter, more conical and elongated inclination. Said to have originated on the Greek island of Cos (Kos) off the coast of Turkey, Romaine or Cos lettuces were known to be under cultivation as early as 3000 B.C. Despite a general belief that the cabbage-headed varieties of the *Lactuca sativa* family are physically closer to their wild Asian ancestors (*Lactuca scariola*), some botanists credit the Cos type with being the oldest form of cultivated lettuce. A famous wall fragment of the third millennium B.C., portraying Min, Egyptian God of fertility and bounty, shows him in full phallic salute amid a field of stylized yet readily identifiable Romaines.

This ancient variety, apparently brought into Italy by way of Turkey, was known to the early Romans as Cappadocian Lettuce. A Romaine variety is know to have been introduced into France in the fourteenth century by the prelates of the Roman Catholic Church who, being under the thumb of the French King Louis X, temporarily moved their pontifical seat from Rome to Avignon. Another early strain of this popular cultivar was said to have been carried into France in 1537 by none other than the legendary gourmand Rabelais. There, initially and generally known as Avignon Lettuce, this well-traveled edible plant was subsequently and more widely referred to as Roman Lettuce. By the early seventeenth century, Romaine had found its way into England, where its current appellation was finally adopted, rooted in the French for "Roman Lettuce": *laitue Romaine.*

By 1623 a whole host of Romaine varieties, from light and dark green to red striated, tipped, and spotted, were being described in Europe. *Forellenschluss,* which translates to "speckled like a trout" and is alternately called Troutback Lettuce, is an extremely handsome Austrian heirloom of the red-spotted variety. It features bright, medium green leaves dappled with lively burgundy splotches, looking for all the world like each head has been spattered with a good red wine. There is also a variety called 'Bunte Forellenschluss' which boasts lighter, more yellow-ish leaves with the same splendid maroon dapplings. These exceedingly attractive 8- to 12-inch heads are also notable for their delightfully smooth, buttery flavor as well as for the fact that they hold exceptionally well in the heat.

Lettuces are mainly cool-weather creatures and fairly undemanding in terms of soil and fertilization although, being 98 percent water, they are tender beings when it comes to drying out, so do keep them evenly moist, particularly at seedling stage. In any case, direct sow or plant out after danger of frost and re-sow at monthly intervals throughout the summer. You should be harvesting these spectacularly speckled leaves about 55 days from sowing, so why not employ them in a newfangled look at a classic salad à la Caesar? In short, whisk up a good Caesar dress-ing with olive oil, egg yolk, mashed anchovy, lemon juice, garlic, salt, pepper, and grated *parmesano* in the bottom of your best wooden salad bowl, then toss with a fresh amplitude of torn Forellenschluss leaves and some garlicky croutons.

ॐ

LETTUCE 'FORELLENSCHLUSS'

Lollo Rossa Lettuce

❧ 41. Lollo Rossa Lettuce ❧
Lactuca sativa

In the ancient Babylonian cult of Ishtar, Queen of the Heavens, and Thammuz, God of the Tigris and Euphrates, who happened to be not only her husband but son and brother all conveniently rolled into one, it is believed that, when Thammuz died, he was laid out by Ishtar on a luxuriant bed of lettuce, an honor bestowed by high-end restaurants on their choicest cuts of beef to this day.

Oddly, although wild lettuces (*Lactuca scariola*) are anciently native to Asia, most cultivated varieties of lettuce did not find their way into China in particular until about the fifth century A.D. However, Asia is home to a venerable lettuce cultivar not found anywhere else on earth. This variety, called 'Stem' or 'Asparagus' Lettuce (*Lactuca angustana*), remarkable for its long, narrow leaves and thick, edible stalks, is, along with the two original forms of the *Lactuca sativa* family, the cabbage-headed, or loose-leaved, type (also known as "Butterheads") and the "Cos" or "Romaine" variety, one of the three earliest descendants of wild lettuce. This robust trio was joined in the early twentieth century by a fourth form: the crisp head variety of *Lactuca sativa,* of which the dangerously ubiquitous "Iceberg" is probably the best known. Although of somewhat suspect taste and texture in comparison to most of the aptly named Butterheads, a wedge of Iceberg with a generous dollop of original Maytag Blue is still a summertime delight at which one is wise not to sneeze.

It was Columbus who introduced the *Lactuca sativa* family to the New World when he landed on Isabella Island in the Bahamas in 1494. Lettuce was a popular edible crop in Haiti by 1565, under cultivation in Brazil before 1650, and could be found growing in every European colony in North America by the end of the seventeenth century. This rapid popularity was due not only to lettuce's unique cooling crispness and short maturation time, but also to its wide usage as a medicinal plant, Thomas Johnson in *The Herball* of 1633, reporting that lettuce "beaten and applied . . . is good against burnes and scaldes . . . procureth sleepe, asswages paine . . . and is drunke against the stingings of scorpions," and John Gerard, in his *Herball* of 1699, asserting that it: "cooleth the heat of the stomacke . . . helpeth it when it is troubled with choler . . . quencheth thirst and causeth sleep."

There is an almost infinite number of lettuces whose physical attributes are commendable, the *Lactuca* family offering up a remarkable variety of beautiful shadings, cuttings, and frilly curlings for the aesthetically inclined gardener to contemplate. Lollo Rossa, an Italian heirloom variety, is certainly one of the most fetching, being possessed of a springy green interior with an intense, rosy, Bordeaux-red coloration on the edges, the leaves themselves being deeply curled and frilled and forming very appealing, loose, 5- to 8-inch heads. Lollo Rossa is also an excellent choice as a baby lettuce as well as a cut-and-come-again variety, and is well known for its mild, sweet flavor and subtly crisp texture.

Direct sow or transplant out in early spring and again in late summer for a fall crop, thinning seedlings to 8 inches apart. You can start cutting the pretty leaves in about 30 days and full-sized heads in about 55. Lollo Rossa would be a really eye-catching variety to chiffonade over a brothy shrimp-and-sea-scallop soup: just add a couple of handfuls of the shredded leaves at the very end of cooking and the heat of the broth will poach them to perfection.

❦ 42. Malabar Spinach ❦
Basella alba rubra

In its native India, an extract of the fruits of the Basella alba *var.* rubra, *the red-stemmed variety of Malabar Spinach, has been employed for countless centuries as both a carmine dye for official seals and a pleasingly natural form of rouge.*

Indigenous to India, Africa, and other parts of Southeast Asia, Malabar Spinach has always conjured up for me images of lush jungles, jeweled idols, and swirling veils of rainbow silk. Located on the southwest coast of India in the state of Kerala, the Malabar region is in fact a land of dense tropical jungle and thriving coconut and pepper plantations, and has most certainly had a long, rich, jewel-bedecked history of Brahmin rule, multiple colorful emperors, religious and social upheaval, and even imperialist invasion, most notably by the Portuguese in the fifteenth century, the Dutch in the seventeenth, and the British in the nineteenth century.

Unlike many other food plant families, the *Basella* clan is an extremely small one and, in fact, one could almost say that Malabar Spinach is an only child, although it does come in both red- and white-stemmed varieties. For some unknown and extremely roundabout reason, the red-stemmed variety of Malabar Spinach is classified as *Basella alba* var. *rubra,* meaning "the red variety of white Basella."

Also known as Ceylon Spinach, East Indian Spinach, Malabar Nightshade, Land Kelp, and Vine Spinach, Malabar Spinach does have one distant South American cousin, known botanically as *Ullucus tuberosus,* or Tuberous *Basella.* An ancient cultivar enjoyed by the Incas, this plant was grown for its potato-like tuber and is still procurable in Peru in long, curved, round, spotted, streaked, yellow and pink varieties.

Malabar Spinach first made its way from India to Europe in 1688, when it was introduced into Holland by the Dutch governor of Malabar,

Malabar Spinach

who had noticed the natives' taste for it. Known continentally from that moment as Malabar Spinach, this fascinating tropical cultivar was introduced into England in the early eighteenth century, but, perhaps because of its long growing season and climatic fussiness, it was not greeted with much enthusiasm and is still relatively unknown outside of its countries of origin. This is decidedly tragic, as Malabar Spinach is a uniquely striking vegetable plant worthy of a place in every potager.

Unlike any spinach you've ever seen, Malabar Spinach is an extremely vigorous viner that can grow to 30 feet or more in length. Although the *alba* variety is quite attractive, it is the var. *rubra* that has the real personality, boasting succulent, deep rhubarb-red vines covered with glossily handsome, crinkled, heart-shaped, green leaves. As well, this extravagant plant also produces tiny, purple-black fruit and pretty, reddish pink flower racemes late in the season, and the sight of these riotously prolific ruby-toned vines looping and threading their way through a trellis wall or up a tall teepee is truly a magnificent sight, rivaled only by the Hyacinth Bean and some of the Runners for pure, vining presence.

As Malabar Spinach needs a warm soil and 110 days to really produce, start this exotic climber indoors 6 weeks before your last frost, then plant out 2 weeks after, spacing at least 2 feet apart, and providing some expansive trellising. The large, meaty leaves are remarkably spinach-like in flavor, with a slightly seaweedy aspect (thus "Land Kelp"), and the raw leaves and tender, young stems are wonderful in salads. For a nice Asian-influenced summer accompaniment, I advise steaming some of these remarkably succulent leaves with some diced tofu and ginger, thus providing a pleasing bed of spicy greens for a briefly poached fish.

ॐ

43. Melon 'Queen Anne's Pocket'
Cucumis melo dudaim

"All of Renaissance France smelled of melon."

—Francois de Malherbe, French Poet Laureate (1555–1628)

There is still some lingering debate over the exact origins of the melon, various clacks championing the arid savannahs of such diverse locales as Persia, Afghanistan, Africa, and Armenia. We do know that melons were cultivated in Babylonia in 2000 B.C. and that the Babylonian king Gilgamesh, hero of the epic Sumerian poem of the same name, was fond of them. The Assyrian king Merodach-Baladan was known to grow them in his gardens as well in the seventh century B.C., and when Moses led the Hebrew people into the desert, where they were destined to wander for a rather trying forty years, one of the foods they craved was melons, Numbers 11:5 reporting that they longed for "the fish, which we did eat in Egypt freely; the cucumbers, and the melons."

We know that melons entered the Mediterranean region in the last century B.C. with the Moors bound for Andalusia, a wall painting depicting melons and dating to around the birth of Christ having been unearthed from the ruins of Herculaneum, the ancient Roman city buried in A.D. 79 in the same Vesuvian eruption that killed the Roman botanist Pliny. By the second century A.D., Galen, the Greek physician and herbalist, was debating the medicinal benefits of melons. Melons were introduced to the New World by way of Haiti in 1494 on Columbus's second voyage, although squash (*Cucumis pepo*), a kissing cousin of the melon, had been growing in the Americas for millennia. By the seventeenth century, melons were under extravagant cultivation in both France and Italy, the French calling them 'Sucrin' for their sweetness, and Jean de la Quintinie, gardener to Louis XIV, planting seven varieties in the *potager du Roi* at Versailles.

The charmingly named 'Queen Anne's Pocket,' also known equally quaintly as the 'Plum Granny,' is a *Cucumis melo dudaim* variety, *dudaim* being the Hebrew word for fruit. This dainty melon cultivar, thought to be Persian by birth and brought to England from Portugal by a General Dormer at the turn of the eighteenth century, produces exceedingly pretty, small round fruit growing to about 3 inches with a velvety skin marked longitudinally with jagged stripes of bright yellow and dark orange. When ripe, the 'Queen Anne's Pocket' is also possessed of a fragrance so legendarily sweet that this winsome creature's common name derives from the fact that Queen Anne of England (1665–1714), in an era not known for its attention to hygiene, was given to carrying one tucked into her pocket as a perfumed sachet. The name "Plum Granny" is a bit more arcane in derivation, although it was known to originate in the Ozarks with settlers who carried seed there from the eastern United States.

Melons, in the main, need a long, hot season and, when at the seedling stage, a steady supply of water. In the North, start melons indoors about 4 weeks prior to planting out when soil temperature hits 60 degrees. Many growers rely on black plastic ground cover and floating row covers to boost heat and water retention: this is a personal call entirely. Charles Estienne, the eighteenth-century French publisher, thought the secret to growing sweet melons was to water them "with honeyed or sweetened water." Also a personal call. The light, almost honeydew-like flavor and diminutive size of the Queen Anne's Pocket make it a perfect choice for scooping out and filling with individual portions of a fresh, icy melon *granitée* of a summer's eve.

MELON 'QUEEN ANNE'S POCKET'

❊ 44. Merlot Lettuce ❊
Lactuca sativa

"He has sprouted; he has burgeoned;
He is lettuce planted by the water.
He is the one my womb loves best."

— Sumerian Song, 3000 B.C.

Lettuce has had a hearty and long tradition of both culinary and medicinal usage and, as such, has been held in devotionally high esteem by some of our most notable ancient civilizations. Herodotus of Halicarnassus, who published his famous *History* in 440 B.C. " . . . in the hope of . . . preventing the great and wonderful actions of the Greeks and the Barbarians from losing their due meed of glory . . . ," wrote of lettuce being enjoyed in ancient Persia in 550 B.C. Hippocrates of Chios, the Greek mathematician who squared the circle and duplicated the cube for us, noted the many herbal usages of lettuce in Greece in 430 B.C., as did the great Aristotle in 356 B.C., and Pliny, the venerated natural historian who died in the A.D. 79 eruption of Mount Vesuvius, described no fewer than nine types of lettuce under cultivation before his untimely demise.

Lettuce's popular history of medicinal usage typically took one of two directions: its employment as a sleep-inducing aid, and its ability to "cool and refresh" both mind and body. Greek myth recounts that, when Adonis died, Venus threw herself onto a bed of lettuce to both lull her grief and cool her desire. John Evelyn makes reference to lettuce's most prevalent uses as well as the poignant denouement of the mythic lovers in his *Acetaria* of 1699, reporting: "Lettuce, *Lactuca:* Tho' by metaphor call'd *'Mortuorum Cibi,'* [to say nothing of Adonis and his sad mistress] by reason of its soporiferous quality, ever was and still continues the principal foundation of the universal tribe of sallets; which is to cool and refresh. . . ."

There are hundreds of varieties of cultivated lettuce, scores of them notable for their variously commendable physical attractions, with red-tinged lettuces having been known since the earliest days of cultivation. Vilmorin-Andrieux mentions numerous red-spotted, striated, dappled, and tipped forms of both the Cabbage-Headed and Cos varieties in *The Vegetable Garden* of 1885, however, not a one of these could truly be called utterly red. Today, varieties with names like 'Red Velvet,' 'Rossimo' and 'Outredgeous' vie for the uniformly carmine crown but a truly, really consistently and deeply red lettuce is still a rarity and, as such, the gorgeous variety "Merlot" is worthy of our undivided attention.

Merlot is a relatively new hybrid lettuce of such dramatic and homogenous deep burgundy intensity, its only crimson competition in the garden will be the Ruby Cabbages, burgundy-plumaged Beets, and some of the Amaranths and Orachs you plant. In any case, do find a place for this indisputable garden dazzler, as it is sure to sound a brilliant and virtually peerless ruby-toned note in any vegetable plot. These dramatically scarlet, medium-sized beauties have a prettily ruffled, loose-leaf habit, growing to about 8 inches in diameter, and possess the additional benefits of a slow bolting demeanor and excellent suitability to cut-and-come-again culture.

Direct sow Merlot in early spring ⅛ inch deep, ultimately thinning to 8 inches apart, or start inside and plant out after danger of frost. In general, lettuce sowed in hot weather goes to seed quickly, though this vivacious cultivar is more bolt-resistant than most, but do cut or pick often once the leaves reach their desired size. Also, planting lettuces in partial shade will help retard midsummer bolting. I'll take these dressed simply with a good Dijon vinaigrette, a dusting of crumbled blue cheese and a handful of golden raisins.

MERLOT LETTUCE

MIZUNA

❧ 45. Mizuna ❧
Brassica rapa Rapifera japonica

In 1845, the Oriental mustards and cabbages introduced into France by that country's most prominent seedsman were met with such supreme indifference that the whole family of plants was ultimately lost and had to be entirely reintroduced later in the century.

The lovely Japanese vegetable plant mizuna is another good example of the rather ambiguous categorization of the vast *Brassica* clan of Oriental leaf mustards, cabbages, and greens. Mizuna, commonly considered an Oriental mustard, rather than being classified as the prototypical *Brassica Luncea,* is labeled *Brassica rapa Rapifera* var. *japonica,* which positions it as a relative of both our common turnip and the *Brassica rapa Sylvestris,* or yellow field mustard, which habitually paints the meadows of Europe with acid summer color. Western botanists have struggled for years to produce an orderly symmetry out of this mess of native Asian cole crops, but with only mixed success. Currently, modern botany divides the *Brassica rapa* family into five substantial subgroups, although there is still considerable crossover and debate: the *Chinensis* Group, which includes Pak-Choi; the *Pekinensis* or Chinese Cabbage Group; the *Perviridis* Group of which spinach mustard is a member; the *Rapifera* or Turnip Group; and the *Ruvo* Group, which consists mainly of *Ruvo* Kale and Broccoli Raab.

This remarkable clan of Far Eastern coleworts, only distantly related to the varieties anciently native to the European continent and possessed of an astonishing diversity of leaf shapes, growth patterns, and intensities of taste, is believed by some to have actually originated in Africa. However, they have been native to Asia for endless millennia, which is one reason for the incredible multiplicity of their forms and habits, which can range from a plant resembling a tight-headed cabbage to another approximating a dandelion on steroids. A good number of these Asian cultivars were introduced, first into the Middle East and India and then into Europe, in the fifteenth through eighteenth centuries, but they never achieved their just culinary due until far more recently.

For a garden green that is basically of an unobtrusive, middle-toned verdure, Mizuna is certainly one of the most durable and handsome. Beautiful, tasty, and prolific, this feathery Japanese "mustard" boasts long, delicate, dramatically cut leaves and graceful stems growing in loosely held crowns to about a foot tall and broad. In these global times, from spring through summer, the jaggedy elegance of bunches of Mizuna leaves can be found in farmers' and Asian markets coast to coast, and they are often included in the mesclun mixes so popularly available these days. As well, they are so decorative as to be commonly used in Japan as an elegant bedding plant that is said to "float" in a flowerbed.

Mizuna is enormously temperature- and soil-tolerant as well, and plants will not only germinate under cold and wet spring conditions, but withstand all but the most intense heat of summer without bolting. Mizuna also seems content to grow in a wide range of soil types, but if it has a preference, it would be for a rich, loamy soil with high water retention. Therefore, direct sow ⅛ inch deep, thinning to 10 to 12 inches, in monthly intervals from spring through September, and you can be harvesting young leaves for salads about three weeks from germination. The taste of Mizuna is mustardy but of a gratifyingly sweet and mild personality so, for a light and zesty meal, try tossing a chopped handful or two of these graceful greens into a shrimp stir-fry, along with some fresh, slivered garlic and ginger, and a few shakes of soy sauce.

❦ 46. Nutri-Red Carrot ❦
Daucus carota sativus

Carrots were so highly valued as an aphrodisiac in ancient Roman that, in a memorable instance of voyeuristic extremity, the Emperor Caligula invited the entire Roman senate to dine and fed them a banquet composed solely of carrot cuisine, so that he might have occasion to observe them "rutting like animals."

Carrots are so unbelievably old that fossil pollen dating from the Eocene Era (a mere 55 million years ago) has been identified as belonging to a member of the carrot family, other more recent relatives including celery, anise, caraway, dill, fennel, parsley, parsnip, Queen Anne's Lace, and poison hemlock. Most historians believe the carrot originated in what is now Afghanistan, although ancient seeds have been found as far afield as the prehistoric lake dwellings in Switzerland and the eighth century B.C. hanging gardens of Babylon, evidence showing, however, that the Babylonians cultivated carrots not for their edible roots but, rather, for their pleasingly aromatic foliage. Egyptian tomb paintings dating to 2000 B.C. frequently portray a plant now thought by many experts to be a purple carrot and, today, wild carrots can still be found growing throughout Europe, Western Asia, Afghanistan, and Turkey.

The carrot migrated westward with travelers and traders from Arabia into the Mediterranean countries and, by the eighth century, the French Emperor Charlemagne was growing carrots in his imperial potager. By the thirteenth century, the carrot had set roots in India and the Far East and, by the fourteenth, was under cultivation in the Netherlands and Germany, finally making its way into England with flemish refugees in the fifteenth century, during the reign of Elizabeth I. By the very early sixteenth century, carrots had found their way to the New World as well, a cultivated

NUTRI-RED CARROT

variety being found already growing on an island off the coast of Venezuela when the island was rediscovered in 1565.

During their long history, carrots appeared in an astounding range of hues, from purple, green, red, and black, to pale yellow and white. In fact, one the few colors carrots did not seem to come in was orange. Bizarrely, the familiar orange root was first bred by the fastidiously patriotic Dutch, who, crossing pale yellow types with anthocyanin-rich red ones in the sixteenth century, refined cultivars to grow in the heraldic colors of their ruling House of Orange. The Nutri-Red Carrot, a modern descendant of one of those ancient crimson varieties, is an extremely striking cultivar: an "Imperatore" type boasting a ravishingly deep scarlet-toned root growing straight as a dagger to a substantial 8 inches, and topped with a finely cut froth of bright green foliage. Additionally, the darker the carrot, the higher its lycopene content, lycopene being thought to be a powerful cancer preventive, so this stunning carmine creature also lives up to its "nutritious" name.

Carrots are relatively carefree and will thrive in any sunny spot with deep, moist, sandy soil to allow for uninterrupted root growth. Direct sow seeds in early spring, thinning to 1 inch apart, and you should be harvesting these robust red roots in about 74 days. Nutri-Red's flavor and color are wonderfully maximized with cooking, so why not follow the example of England's Elizabeth I who, when presented by the Dutch ambassador with a tribute of a diamond-studded wreath of carrots and a tub of butter from Holland, plucked off the diamonds and rushed the carrots and butter off to the kitchen, giving birth to the classic dish of boiled, buttered carrots. Add a sprinkle of chopped, fresh dill to give it a regal touch all your own.

❦ 47. Okra 'Red Burgundy' ❦
Hibiscus esculentus

Okra's rather mucilaginous reputation is due to the acetylated acidic polysaccharides and galaturonic acids it contains: it releases these slippery compounds when cut, making it the wildly popular thickener of gumbos and stews it has become.

Ancient varieties of okra can still be found growing wild from Ethiopia to the White Nile in Egypt, and this interesting food plant is believed to have originated in Ethiopia. In the absence of any ancient Indian names for it, modern botanists believe that it found its way to India after the dawn of the Christian Era in about A.D. 200, then wended its way across the Red Sea into Arabia. As both the Moors and Egyptians of the twelfth century A.D. employed the Arab word for okra, it was then probably transported into Egypt by the invading Muslims around the seventh century A.D. Some of the earliest mentions of okra were noted by a Spanish Moor who, traveling with the great warrior prince Saladin during the Crusades, saw it growing in Egypt in A.D. 1216.

Okra was introduced to the New World sometime before 1658 and most probably reached Brazil and Dutch Guiana with slaves from the Gold Coast of Africa. The okra brought in by slaves from Angola was natively called *ochinggombo,* which was later shortened to *ngombo,* then *gombo,* finally evolving into the familiar *gumbo,* a term which stood for both the native stew they enjoyed as well as the vegetable it still so famously contains. In North America, okra was grown as far north as Philadelphia by 1748, and Thomas Jefferson noted it at Monticello in 1781. From about 1800 onwards, okra was a plant staple of the American South, and several distinct varieties were under cultivation as early as 1806.

Okra is a member of the Mallow family (*Hibiscus esculentus*), and, as such, is related to cotton, the hibiscus, and the hollyhock. Even in its usual green form, it's a tall, handsome plant with nicely-cut leaves and large, yellow, hibiscus-like flowers, cultivated for its edible seed pods, which are elegantly curved and finger-like, pointed at the extremity, the stem end appearing to wear a pretty conical cap. It is the 'Red Burgundy' Okra, however, bred by Leon Robbins of Clemson University, about which we choose to wax poetic in this volume. This is an extremely lovely plant, growing to about 4 feet, with stems, fruit, and leaf ribs all being a rich and visually arresting burgundy red, and the leaves a fresh, bright green. The really charming flowers do indeed resemble miniature hibiscus blossoms, boasting sunny, lemon-colored petals and deep ruby throats. All in all, a real stunner in the garden.

Okra is one of those rare tropicals with a short growing season (a mere 60 days to harvest), so direct sow ½ to 1 inch deep when soil is well warmed up, then thin plants to 12 inches apart. Okra is also a vegetable variety really undeserving of its oft-maligned culinary possibilities, the first mistake most gardeners make being to let the pods become too old and tough before harvesting. Okra grows rapidly and should be picked when seedpods are only 4 inches or so in length, about 4 to 5 days after flowering. The second mistake most cooks make is to overcook okra into slimy submission. Okra actually has a wonderful flavor, somewhere between asparagus and eggplant, and a natively crisp demeanor. Do like they do down South and simply slice into bite-sized disks, dredge in cornmeal with a dash of salt and pepper, and fry. I promise you'll be delighted at the tasty result.

OKRA 'RED BURGUNDY'

❧ 48. Oraꞔh 'Crimson Plume' ❧
Atriplex hortensis rubra

*Orach was so highly esteemed a food plant by ancient Arabic cultures
that they referred to it as "the prince of vegetables."*

Among the oldest of cultivated, edible plants, Orach is thought to
have originated in the region of the fertile Oxus Valley, believed
by many to be the original site of the Garden of Eden, on what
is now the Pakistan/Afghanistan border. Introduced into Spain in the
eleventh century by Arab traders moving northward along the silk
roads, Orach reached southern Europe with the returning Crusaders in
the thirteenth century and, by the fourteenth century, Buddhist monks
were known to be cultivating it in China. Its arrival in England was documented in 1548 and by 1699 it had earned the praise of the herbalist John
Evelyn, who noted that: "Orache is cooling (and) allays the Pituit
Humor."

Orach is a member of the goosefoot or *Chenipodiae* family and, therefore, related to our common Lamb's Quarters, or "Pigweed," and the
Amaranths. Like many ancient vegetable plants, Orach was commonly
prescribed for a whole panoply of early bodily afflictions, ranging from
employment as a diuretic, purgative, and emetic, to a poultice for the
gout, to a liniment and emollient recommended for "indurations and
tumors," particularly of the throat. Also know as "Mountain Spinach,"
the name "Orach" is actually a corruption of the Latin *aurum* or "gold,"
because its seeds, when mixed with wine, were also a popular medieval
cure for yellow jaundice.

There are a number of varieties of Orach of various colorations, a
total of seven being listed by Fearing Burr in his *The Field and Garden
Vegetables of America* in 1865. The red form was first documented in
the New World by John Lawson, Surveyor General of North Carolina,
in his *History of Carolina* of 1714, and was listed by Bernard McMahon in

his *American Gardener's Calendar* by 1806. Thomas Jefferson was known to have the green form under cultivation at Monticello at about the same time. The white and green forms are popularly considered to be the most desirable culinarily, but here I commend the dramatic and vivacious 'Crimson Plume' form.

This elegant cultivar is so attractive, one often sees it in mixed English borders for its sheer physical splendor. Every part of this lovely plant, including leaves, stalks, and stems, is a deep, regal burgundy, the whole growing straight and slim to 3 or 4 feet and topped with a feathery and highly decorative crimson seed head. Companioned with contrasting edible foliage plants, Orach Crimson Plume is a worthy visual addition to any vegetable garden. Like other tropical spinach cultivars, Orachs like a warm, sunny aspect, although, once established, they are surprisingly drought- and soil-tolerant. Therefore, direct seed when soil is well warmed up, thinning to about a foot apart for a nice, thick patch, and water generously at the seedling stage, and you should be harvesting in 40 to 60 days.

Much like the amaranth, the leaves of Orach Crimson Plume are rich in calcium and vitamins A and C, best picked when young to obtain optimum tenderness and flavor, and can be used fresh or cooked as a spinach substitute. In 1699, however, John Evelyn reported that "the tender leavers are mingl'd with other cold Salleting; but 'tis better in Pottage." Therefore, while a few crimson leaves will certainly add a colorful note to a summer salad, why not swirl a chiffonade of these pretty carmine leaves into a hot, nourishing consommé, topped with a dollop of sour cream?

ॐ

ORACH 'CRIMSON PLUME'

OSTEREI EGGPLANT

❦ 49. Osterei Eggplant ❦
Solanum melongena

". . . greedily they pluck'd
The Frutage fair to sight, like that which grew
Neer that bituminous Lake where SODOM flam'd;
This more delusive, not the touch, but taste
Deceav'd; they fondly thinking to allay
Their appetite with gust, instead of Fruit
Chewd bitter Ashes, which th' offended taste
With spattering noise rejected . . ."

— John Milton, *Paradise Lost,* 1687

The eggplant is interestingly possessed of one of the most distinguished and curious literary provenances of any vegetable genus. Because of its *Solanum* roots and, therefore, close kinship to nightshade, the eggplant was known across many early cultures as the "madde" or "rage" apple, and, consequently, was thought to induce madness and even death. Additionally, because eggplants were believed to have originated near the Dead Sea and the imagined site of Sodom and Gomorrah, they were also known popularly, or perhaps unpopularly, as "apples of Sodom." Josephus, the ancient Jewish historian, wrote that he had himself seen the beautiful purple "apples of Sodom" which, magically and clearly with divine purpose, vanished in smoke when they touched one's lips. This bit of ancient lore was also employed by John Milton in *Paradise Lost,* when he spoke of the singularly disappointing diet of the fallen angels.

Oddly, this fanciful legend of shining *aubergine* skin cloaking an interior of bitter ashes may be based in fact. Excavated remains have revealed that, very possibly, it was an invasive insect that begot this particular brand of heavenly magic, boring into the flesh of the eggplant and causing it to powder and decay interiorly while the skin remained beautifully intact. Thus, it would seem it was entirely possible to bite into what appeared to be a glossy bit of heaven only to come up with a mouthful of everlasting repentance. Although this early lore refers to a purple-fruited plant, the most common early type was, in fact, a small, oval, white fruit so closely resembling a hen's egg that the genus, as a whole, assumed the name.

Also known as the 'Easter Egg' or 'White Egg' eggplant, the Osterei Eggplant will provide you with an abundance of enchanting, oval-shaped, white-skinned fruit that really do look like remarkably like their fowl-generated doubles. The plant itself is attractively low-growing and branching with green stem and leafstalks, often faintly tinged with purple, and the flowers are a lovely, soft lilac.

Vilmorin-Andrieux listed this variety as "white eggplant" (*solanum ovigerun*), and described it as "exactly resembling a hen's egg" but considered it "more ornamental than useful," and further described it as "considered by some to be unwholesome." As in many modern civilizations, however, it seemed that others were rushing to embrace this unwholesomeness, and white eggplant was listed along with a purple variety in several eastern United States seed catalogues by 1825. Thomas Jefferson was growing both types at Monticello by 1812 and by 1863, Fearing Burr was calling the Osterei Eggplant "the earliest, hardiest and most productive of all the varieties."

Eggplants are tropical plants that love heat. Don't rush to put them out in spring and, in cooler climates, you can lay black plastic over the beds two weeks before setting out your transplants to preheat the soil. Space plants 15 inches apart in rows, and if temperatures are expected to dip below 60 degrees, cover the plants with floating row covers. While this original form of eggplant is thought by some to be somewhat lackluster in taste, it is also considered by many to be the superior culinary type, in part because of its thin, edible skin when picked white. Try it cubed, sautéed with garlic, olive oil, salt, and pepper, then tossed with cherry tomatoes, crumbled gorgonzola, fresh, chopped mint, and a splash of balsamico for a fantastic, tepid summer salad.

❧ 50. Painted Serpent Cucumber ❧
Cucumis melo

"The fruit . . . made into a potage with oatmeal, where of a messes eaten to breakfast, as much to dinner, and the like to supper . . . doth perfectly cure all manner of sauce flegme and copper faces, red and shining fierie noses as red as red roses, with pimples, pumples, rubies and such like precious faces."

— John Gerard, *The Herball*, 1636

Historically, cucumbers are singular among vegetables for having been esteemed not only as things *of* beauty, but *for* it as well. As early as the seventeenth century, John Gerard was extolling their benefits to troublesome complexions, and today the beauty industry still employs cucumber extracts in a variety of soothing skincares: try, for instance, a slice simply laid on tired eyes for instant refreshment. However, and in a typical early dichotomy of herbal opinion, the early Greeks named the cucumber *sikys,* signifying that the plant sadly lacked aphrodisiac qualities, while old English herbals recommended that any woman who wished for children should wear a cucumber strategically suspended from her girdle. Each, apparently, to her own.

Cultivated cucumbers were certainly known in Italy by the second century B.C. when Marcus Terentius Varro gave this fruit the Latin name of *Curvimur,* referring to the usual curvature of its form. In France, the cucumber was listed in the *Capitulare de Villis* in the eighth century A.D., when it was a favorite of the Emperor Charlemagne, and it was most probably introduced into England in the fourteenth century during the reign of Edward III. Somehow, it seems, the cucumber was then misplaced by the English during the War of the Roses, but was happily reintroduced there during the reign of Henry VIII with the advent of the Spanish-born Catherine of Aragon, who liked them in her salads.

PAINTED SERPENT CUCUMBER

Columbus introduced the cucumber to Haiti in 1494, and just fifteen years later DeSoto reported seeing them in Florida.

It is thought by most that the modern cucumber is a descendant of the wild *Cucumis harwickii,* a scraggly, spiny, bitter-fruited native of the foothills of the Himalayas. The Painted Serpent Cucumber (*Cucumis melo*), also known as the Armenian Striped and Chinese Sweet Cucumber, is an Oriental type (long, thin, small-seeded, with a tendency to be ridged and curled) and therefore, in fact, technically a melon (thus *melo*). However, as they taste like a cucumber, have virtually the same growth habits, and are eaten as a vegetable not a fruit, we choose to call them one. What is most striking about this spectacular cultivar, however, is its signature, long, curling habit and bold green- and white-striped ribs, and it is often discovered curled amidst its pretty leaves looking exactly like its dramatic namesake.

Like all cucumbers and melons, this one will do best in well-warmed-up, free-draining soil, so in the North, start seeds in the greenhouse in May and transplant out in June. As the fruit develops, keep it picked to keep plants producing, and do provide some stout trellising so these fantastic fruits can twist into their truly exceptional forms. The thin skin, which means no peeling necessary, and lack of seeds of the Painted Serpent also render them virtually "burpless" and free of bitterness, with a crisp demeanor and delicate, slightly sweet taste. They also happen to slice into perfect scallops, so try slicing these an inch thick, sautéing in a bit of butter with chopped, fresh tarragon until tender, then tossing until warmed with a splash of cream, salt, and pepper. This makes a particularly delicious, subtle accompaniment to a roast fish or hen.

PRESCOTT FOND BLANC MELON

✳ 51. Prescott Fond Blanc Melon ✳
Cucumis melo

"He who fills his stomach with melons is like he who fills it with light — there is a blessing in them."

— Middle Eastern Proverb

Cantaloupes have been cultivated in Egypt, Iran, and India since prebiblical times and are thought to be native to Armenia. Journeying north with the Moors by the first century A.D., Pliny, the Roman naturalist, reports on a spherical, yellowish, cucumber-esque thing growing on a crawling vine, which detaches easily from its stem, which he called *melopepo,* now believed to be an early cantaloupe. Albertus Magnus, the thirteenth century German alchemist and saint, certainly describes the cantaloupe as *pepo,* the common European term, although, oddly, this particular piece of nomenclature now belongs to the melon's American cousins, the squash (*Cucumis pepo*) and pumpkin (*Cucurbita pepo*).

Cantaloupes acquired their current common name in the sixteenth century, when melon seeds from Armenia were carried by missionaries to Cantalupo (Italian for "Singing Wolf"), the country residence of the Pope near Tivoli outside of Rome, and planted them in the papal gardens. There are seven different botanical variations on the cantaloupe theme, including the *Reticulatus* (our familiar cantaloupe), Galia, Persian, Charentais, and *Cantaloupensis,* the true cantaloupe, which has a completely different appearance than the rest and is only to be found in Europe.

Cantaloupes were introduced to the New World by Columbus in 1494 and, by the mid-nineteenth century, the Navajos in the North American Southwest were known to be growing them. Our familiar small, spherical American cantaloupe or "muskmelon," sold as 'Netted

Gem' because of its very netted rind, was developed by the Burpee Seed Company in 1881. Named after a British gardener, the "Prescott" family of cantaloupes, also called rock melons, can range from silver to black in color; however, what is most notable about the Prescott clan is the rather fantastic quality of their rind: warted and crumpled and as tough as rhinoceros hide. The Prescott Fond Blanc ("white bottom"), once a favorite of French market gardeners, is a glorious French heirloom Prescott with a white rind.

Dr. Amy Goldman, curbit authority and author of *Melons for the Passionate Grower,* gives a marvelous description of this fabulous cultivar: "This ethereal, deeply furrowed, puffy-looking melon reminds me of dough rising — I love to run my fingers over its wrinkled, warted, rock-hard shell and to smell true cantaloupe . . . . " Like other cantaloupes, Prescott Fond Blancs are borne on stout vines with handsome, deeply cut green leaves, and bloom with pretty yellow blossoms. As well, like all cantaloupes, the Prescott Fond Blanc is extremely low in calories, has almost zero fat, and provides healthy doses of vitamins A and C, potassium, an important anticoagulant called adenosine, and, like other orange-fleshed vegetables, a good dollop of the anticarcinogen beta-carotene.

Cantaloupes thrive best in hot climes, although it is interesting to note that, in 1895, Colorado was the home of the first, real large-scale American cantaloupe industry. At any rate, since they are mainly heat loving (and, therefore, very frost sensitive), start seeds in seed cups in the greenhouse 2 or 3 weeks before your last frost; then don't plant out till 2 weeks after, when soil temperatures should hopefully have reached 60 degrees. While leaner of flesh than some other modern melons, the interior of the Prescott Fond Blanc is as notable as its unique exterior, being exceedingly sweet and aromatic, so why not savor this ambrosial, orange flesh by cutting yourself a lavish wedge, sprinkling a bit of lemon juice for contrast, and grabbing a spoon?

ॐ

❦ 52. Pumpkin 'Baby Boo' ❦
Cucurbita pepo

"For pottage and puddings and custard and pies,
Our pumpkins and parsnip are common supplies:
We have pumpkins at morning and pumpkins at noon,
If it were not for pumpkins, we should be undoon!"

— American Pilgrim Verse, circa 1630

The pumpkin is one of our oldest native American crops, pumpkin seeds having been found both at Machu Pichu and in the caves of the basket-weaving tribes of Colorado and Arizona dating to 2000 B.C. Native Americans believed pumpkins had been brought to earth by the "Great Spirit" or "Maize Mother," who walked the fields and plains in human form, causing maize to grow from her footsteps and pumpkins and squash plants to sprout in her wake. In 1529, Hernando DeSoto reported from Tampa Bay, Florida, that: "Beans and pumpkins were in great plenty. Both are larger and better than those of Spain; the pumpkins when roasted had nearly the taste of chestnuts."

As we all know, pumpkins were also among the foodstuffs served at the Pilgrims' first Thanksgiving and, in fact, for many years, members of the Church of England referred to Thanksgiving derisively as "St. Pompion's Day," *pompion* being the Old English nomenclature for the pumpkin. Edward Johnson, in his *Wonder Working Providence of Scion's Saviour in New England* of 1654, wrote that the pumpkin was "a fruit which the Lord fed his people with till corn and cattle increased," and the pumpkin was so widely regarded as a food crop in the Massachusetts colonies that Boston, before it was called Beantown, was known as Pumpkinshire.

By 1780, Yale students were referring to all New Englanders as "Pumpkin Heads," another derisive term derived from the law that

PUMPKIN 'BABY BOO'

required men's haircuts to conform to a cap placed over the head, the ubiquitous pumpkin shell often, apparently, being substituted for the far scarcer caps. Size also seems to have been a lifelong issue with the pumpkin in America, as, in 1699, Massachusetts farmer Paul Dudley boasted of having produced a specimen weighing 260 pounds and, in 1721, Joshua Hempsted of Connecticut noted in his farm diary: "Wednesday, 20th: saw a pumpkin 5 foot 11 inches round."

The cultivar we recommend here, the delightful 'Baby Boo,' is a pumpkin at entirely the other end of the dimensional spectrum. A miniature modern hybrid, 'Baby Boo' weighs in at a tiny 2 to 3 inches around, with a true, squat, deeply ribbed, classic pumpkin shape. It is its coloration, however, that makes it genuinely remarkable, as, true to its name, this little darling is a ghostly white in hue. There is simply nothing prettier than to allow a vine or two of tiny 'Baby Boos' to clamber up a trellis, the strikingly pale, tennis-ball-sized fruit brilliant against handsome green foliage and so pretty hanging pendant against the blue of sky or the green of other leaves.

'Baby Boo' will grow best in a moist soil with some compost or manure worked into it, and will need about 40 square feet of growing space, which is why I recommend some stout trellising. Therefore, after your frost date, plant 3 seeds together 1 inch deep, keeping them evenly moist and supplying a layer of straw or mulch, then thinning to the single best plant per 5 feet of trellising. Harvest in about 80 days. Why not honor our hospitable Native American ancestors by serving 'Baby Boos' as individual "pompion pies": cut a hole in the top of each, remove the seeds, fill the cavity with chunks of apple, raisins, cinnamon, nutmeg, sugar, and milk, then bake till piping hot?

❧ 53. Purple Calabash Tomato ❧
Solanum lycopersicon esculentum

On September 26, 1820, Colonel Robert Gibbon Johnson, seeking to disprove the theory that the tomato was poisonous, ate a basketful on the steps of the courthouse in Salem, New Jersey, while a firehouse band played dirges and scores of people fainted. Colonel Johnson not only survived the incident but lived to help introduce America to its favorite homegrown food.

North America is notable in two aspects in its relationship with its favorite backyard food crop. First of all, although Cortes saw the tomato growing in Montezuma's garden in Tenochtitlan (now Mexico City) in 1519, this native American cultivar had to make its way home with the Portuguese and the Spanish, and then recross the Atlantic Ocean in the late eighteenth century to find its way to the north of its own continent. It wasn't until 1793 that the great American portraitist Charles Wilson Peale finally received "red tomato" seeds in a shipment of "a number of subjects of natural science" from France and, it wasn't until 1795 that the tomato made its first appearance in North American art in Peale's son Raphaele's "Still Life with Vegetables and Fruit."

The second notable fact concerning North America and the tomato is our initial, total dismissal of this currently favored darling. The Pilgrims were early tomato bashers, considering them "an abomination," and, 200 years later, Joseph T. Buckingham, editor of the *Boston Courier,* was still calling the tomato "the mere fungus of an offensive plant, which one cannot touch without an immediate application of soap and water . . . deliver us, oh, ye caterers of luxuries, ye gods and goddesses of the science of cookery! Deliver us from tomatoes!" Even as late as 1836, a Mr. Wilcox, editor of the *Florida Agriculturist,* pronounced his first tomato "an arrant humbug" that "deserved forthwith to be consigned to the tomb of all the Capulets."

Early tomatoes came in a huge variety of sizes, shapes, and colorations, ranging from currant-sized to 2-pound mammoths, round to "ox-hearted" to totally misshapen, black and dark purple to red and orange, to yellow, and green and white, and they were all either ribbed or lobed or both. In fact, it wasn't until the turn of the eighteenth century that Joseph Pitton de Tournefort, botanist to Louis XIV, described a *Lycopersicum rubro non striato,* or "red wolf's peach without ribs." The Purple Calabash I recommend here is a lovely, big, old-fashioned, deeply fluted, burgundy beauty, looking for all the world like a Cinderella's pumpkin, growing to about 3 inches wide and 2 inches tall. In hue, these fruits gradate becomingly from a light, greeny purple at the shoulders to darker purple at the base, with an equally deeply purple interior. In fact, in terms of intensity of color, tomato aficionados consider the Purple Calabash to be the most dramatically purple tomato they know.

As with all tomatoes, start these indoors 4 to 6 weeks before transplanting out when soil is well warmed up in a well-manured, sunny spot. You can expect large harvests of these ravishing, indeterminate tomatoes in about 90 days from transplant. In terms of taste, the Purple Calabash is thought by many to be one of the most complex, rich, and "winey"-tasting tomatoes you can grow, one writer lauding their "deep swirling tomato flavors," another finding them reminiscent of a "fruity cabernet." I, personally, in deference to the heroic Colonel Johnson, would be tempted to pluck one of these still warm off the vine and, with the greatest relish, sink my teeth into it then and there. You may hold the dirges.

PURPLE CALABASH TOMATO

🎐 54. Purple Sprouting Broccoli 🎐
Brassica oleracea italica

Desperate Mother: "It's broccoli, dear."

Petulant Child: "I say it's spinach and I say the hell with it."

— E. B. White, Cartoonist, *The New Yorker,* 1925

It is widely believed that Sprouting Broccoli is the most ancient form of this specific subspecies of cruciferous vegetable. Pliny the Elder reported that the inhabitants of Rome grew and enjoyed broccoli during the first century B.C., where the most common, green-headed variety, "Calabrese," was first developed. Following its introduction into France by the famously rapacious Catherine de Medici in 1533, broccoli made its way into England, where it was known to the court of Elizabeth I as "brawcle." However, it seems that, in general, the English and French were less than enthusiastic about this new food plant, preferring instead its big-headed *Brassica* cousins, the cabbage and the cauliflower.

Thomas Jefferson recorded a planting of broccoli at Monticello in 1767, and in 1775 John Randolph described it in *A Treatise on Gardening by a Citizen of Virginia,* citing that "the stems will eat like asparagus, and the heads like cauliflower." Despite this heartening description, broccoli was received in North America in much the same fashion as it had been in France and England: with stunning indifference. In fact, it wasn't really until the early twentieth century that broccoli finally took hold in the United States, its ultimately broad introduction and distribution making for a true American success story.

In 1922, the brothers Stephano and Andrea d'Arrigo of Messina, Italy, immigrated to the United States, settling in San Jose, California, and bringing with them some broccoli seeds of the Calabrese variety. Beginning with some trial plantings and the export of a few crates to Boston, they met with surprising success. With their eyes firmly on the

American dream, they established a business they named after Stephano's two-year-old son. In a matter of years, "Andy Boy" Broccoli fairly owned the booming broccoli industry in the United States, where, in the past twenty-five years alone and due in great part to broccoli's now famously vitamin-rich reputation, consumption has increased a stupendous 940 percent.

The ancient Purple Sprouting Broccoli, also called 'Asparagus Broccoli' historically for the many tender shoots it produces, is a tall, sturdy yet elegant plant with pretty, prolifically produced, purple-tinged sprigs borne on handsome, upright green stalks. It's also notable for its excellent flavor and exceptional hardiness, being able to withstand all but the most severe frosts. That said, I have a horrible admission: it is also a variety bred for overwintering and, as such, takes a full 6 months to bear. Therefore, I'm forced to admit that, unless the winter is exceedingly mild, it is inappropriate for culture in our most northerly climes, including my own. However, I am intent on including it in this volume as it is hardy in many of our states, and anyone lucky enough to be able to grow it will be rewarded with the sweetest, most tender, purple-tinged harbingers of spring imaginable, as early as March.

Therefore, those of you with winters that refuse to plunge below 10 degrees may plant in autumn for a spring harvest. Sow in the fall, thin to about 15 inches apart, spread a little mulch around in winter, and look for your just reward in very early spring. The rest of us will just have to forswear growing or hope for extraordinarily clement weather. These lovely sprigs are so tender and delicious, a quick steam, a piece of butter, and a sprinkle each of salt, pepper, and lemon are all that is needed.

PURPLE SPROUTING BROCCOLI

Radish 'Misato Rose'

55. Radish 'Misato Rose'
Raphanus sativus

According to Herodotus, the fifth-century B.C. author of The History, *the first historical narrative to discuss the life and customs of the Middle East and Aegean, the builders of the Great Pyramids of Egypt existed solely on a diet of radishes, garlic, and onion.*

First mentioned in China as early as 1100 B.C. and believed to have originated there, the radish, actually a member of the mustard family, was known and honored as an edible and herbal plant by most of the great old-world civilizations, including those of the Greeks, Romans, and Egyptians. Although the common American variety is fairly uniformly globular and red-skinned, radishes can vary in coloration from white to red to yellow, purple, and black, and can run the gamut of exterior shapes from tiny and round or oval to the huge and parsnip-like.

The radish industry's minimum standard for the common red radish is ⅛ inch in diameter, however, radishes can run anywhere from miniscule globes less than ½ inch around to carrot-like giants such as some of the Asian Daikons, which can grow to a truly impressive 3 feet in length. Interestingly, in comparison to our moderate radish consumption habits, Daikon radishes are so standard a food plant in Japan that they constitute a whopping 25 percent of that country's vegetable crop. In terms of size, ancient Greek and Roman legends tell of radishes weighing 50 pounds or more, and ancient Jewish lore relates the tale of a radish so large that a fox hollowed it out and made a den of it.

Like other mustards, radishes have been employed medicinally across many cultures and for a variety of ailments: in ancient Greece, for instance, a syrup of radishes was recommended for whooping cough and hoarseness. In medieval times, radish-based concoctions were directed for bouts of madness, incidents of satanic temptation, and spells of demonic possession. In the seventeenth- and eighteenth-century slave cultures of the Americas, radish-based potions and tonics were also employed as medications for headaches, joint pain, eye-ache, and weakness of the limbs.

Radishes, like many root vegetables, don't really reveal their most exciting qualities until unearthed. However, the dainty 'Misato Rose' Radish is one of those unassuming, subterranean growers that is surely worth a spot in your garden. Also known as the Chinese Red Heart Radish, this charming cultivar is descriptively known as *xin li mei* or "in one's heart beautiful" in its native country. Growing to a shapely 2 to 4 inches in diameter, the 'Misato Rose' is, exteriorly, a lovely white gradating to pale green with a froth of deeper green at the leaf end, and blushed with rose at the root end. However, bite into this demure beauty and you will reveal a genuinely flamboyant heart of pale rose shot through with dramatic fuchsia pink veining. Absolutely gorgeous.

Radishes are cool-weather crops, and the stunning 'Misato Rose' is no exception, so start these ravishing roots in early spring as soon as ground can be worked and again in midsummer for a fall harvest. Direct sow thinly about ½ inch deep and thin to 6 inches apart, and you should be harvesting in 35 to 55 days. I suggest enjoying the lovely 'Misato Rose' as the French do, served fresh from the garden with a quick rinse, a dish of coarse salt, and a dish of softened, unsalted butter. Grab by the leaves, dip into the butter, then the salt, and enjoy a wonderful, springy symphony of taste and texture.

❧ 56. Redbor Kale ❧
Brassica oleracea acephala

Although broadly regarded as perhaps less than fashionable, kale is con-
sidered by many botanists to be an edible plant of such universal stamina,
adaptability, ease of cultivation, and nutritive value that it is destined
to be a food source of huge global importance in the coming millennia.

If you asked most people to describe kale, they would probably say
something like "a primitive cabbage," and they would be exactly
right, as kale is considered by many to be the original plant form of
the entire *Brassica* family, although some dissenters continue to cast their
vote on the "mustard" side of the line. If one is compelled to give a birthplace to this ancient vegetable dynasty, most will cite Italy and the eastern
Mediterranean. This family is particularly notable for the fact that, since
about the fifth century B.C., and with no knowledge of plant breeding or
genetics, farmers from around the globe refined and selected this crop
based simply on their own particular tastes and eventually developed a
total of no less than six wildly different vegetable varieties, all card-
carrying *Brassica oleraceas*.

The far-flung *Brassica oleracea* family also includes three different
species it calls kale, all probably still extremely close to their wild,
ancient roots. There is the species *Brassica oleracea acephala,* the common
Italian ancestor of cabbage, broccoli, and cauliflower, among others.
Then there is the *Brassica oleracea alboglabra* group, which includes the
pretty, white-flowered Chinese kale. And, finally, there is the species
Brassica oleracea napus, which includes the rutabaga, red Russian kale, and
rape, all widely grown in northern Eurasia. Vilmorin-Andrieux listed a
healthy twenty-six kale varieties in *The Vegetable Garden* of 1885, including
perennial kales; kales with edible trunks; spring, summer, winter, and
fall bearing kales; and kales bred solely for their crisp side shoots.

REDBOR KALE

Redbor, a descendant of one of the native European varieties, is everything you could want in an ornamental vegetable, being movie star—gorgeous, strong as a team of frost-proof oxen, and unbelievably good for you. This fantastic, frost-loving beauty, a dramatically dark red hybrid of the popular, green "Winterbor," is really one of those vegetables pretty enough to pop into a flower border, and it makes a fantastic edging plant for an island bed. Growing to a height of 24 to 26 inches, this burgundy-hued stunner ultimately composes itself into a frilly crown of deeply curled and cut, deep wine-red leaves 12 inches in diameter. And, of course, not content with mere pulchritude like all kales, this one is also packed with vitamins and so hardy that, in many parts of the United States, they will crop right through winter if mulched a tad.

Kale is a fairly short-season vegetable plant that will perform best in cool weather and tolerate a good deal of frost when established. Therefore, in May, after the danger of hard frost has passed, direct sow seed ½ inch deep and about 1 inch apart, then thin to 12 inches between plants after their third true leaf has emerged. Optionally, you can start kale indoors in seed cups for 3 or 4 weeks, then transplant out on a timing to hit a few of your frosty days at the end of the season as a touch of frost always adds to sweetness. Redbor is as versatile a green as spinach, chard, or cabbage: mild and crisp when picked young, let it add a colorful zest to salads, or chiffonade the bigger leaves, steam briefly, and serve with sour cream, caraway seeds, and a good dose of freshly ground black pepper.

🎗 57. Rhubarb Chard 🎗
Beta vulgaris cicla

"A beautiful sort, remarkable for the rich and brilliant color of the stems and nerves of the leaves."

— Fearing Burr, *Field and Garden Vegetables of America,* 1863

C hard was certainly domesticated by as far back as 2000 B.C., joining such other leafy greens as kale, spinach, mustard, and collards as a previously wild and, therefore, extremely antique form of vegetative human fodder. However, in Greece by the fifth century A.D., chard appears to have suffered much the same fate as the common broad bean, its reputedly coarse and fibrous personality edging it perilously close to the classification of animal silage. And so, for a bit, chard was widely thought to be fit only for the "lower orders," who consumed it broadly and famously in a near universal *potage maigre* or "mean soup," usually a hearty amalgam of stewed chard, spinach, cabbage, and sorrel. However, by the Middle Ages, it seemed no meal laid on even the most elevated tables was complete without a chard-based soup, Jean de la Quintinie, gardener to Louis IV at Versailles, reaffirming this in 1693 in his famous *The Compleat Gardener,* recording: "Chard-beets . . . is the true Chard used in pottages."

Chard got its common name over some confusion with another early Mediterranean vegetable, the cardoon. Somehow, the French got the two plants mentally intertangled, both being grown at that time for their tasty midribs, so they were both called "carde" or "chard" from the French *chardon,* meaning "thistle." Clearly, the association is referential to the cardoon, but the name stuck. Chard has been valued throughout its long history as a source of vigor and stamina, having been lauded by Aristotle himself as an invaluable source of physical dynamism. It is, in fact, a powerhouse of nutrients, with impressive concentrations of vitamins A,

C, E, K, and B6, magnesium, potassium, iron, manganese, copper, calcium, phosphorus, zinc, thiamin, niacin, folate, selenium, protein, and fiber. There's no denying it: greens are good for you.

Rhubarb Chard is a most ancient variety, red-ribbed varieties of chard being noted, again, by Aristotle as early as 350 B.C., and in China by the seventh century A.D., although it has certainly undergone refinements over the past millennia. Rhubarb Chard is also an important element in the seed collection known as Rainbow Chard or Chard 'Bright Lights,' comprising the crimson presence in the mix. However, it deserves a place all to itself in this small volume, as a stand of it in the garden is certainly one of the most palpitatingly dramatic color statements you will ever have the chance to make. When the sun shines on this stunning beauty's brilliant ruby stalks and leaf veins, it seems to glow with an almost unearthly phosphorescence of color, providing gorgeous contrast to its glossy, heavily crumpled, lushly green leaves.

As I've mentioned, chard is virtually carefree to cultivate, being one of those hoped-for vegetable varieties characterized by cheerfulness in any kind of soil, quick growth, yields over a long period if frequently cut, and an extremely pleasing flavor. Start in or out until July, planting seeds or seedlings 3 inches apart, then thinning to about 8 inches apart. Tastewise, chard boasts the slight bitterness of beet greens and the somewhat salty flavor of spinach, being a relative of both. Many soup makers marry it to sorrel, which adds a pleasing and balancing acidity. Why not try this particular one made as the French do: braised in a rich stock, drained, then flavored with mashed garlic and anchovies, and a grinding of fresh pepper. Santé!

RHUBARB CHARD

ॐ 58. Royal Oakleaf Lettuce ✢
Lactuca sativa

In ancient Egypt, lettuce, widely associated with fertility and procre-
ation, was frequently offered to the god Min, the priapic deity who ruled
over all vegetation and who, apparently, was especially fond of lettuce
because of the milky sap it produced when squeezed.

The tales of lettuce's soporific qualities are as legendary as they
are far-flung. We know, for instance, that the ancient Greeks
served lettuce soup at the end of the meal in order to better
guide their guests along the path to dreamland. Conversely, the Emperor
Domitian, who was perhaps justly assassinated in A.D. 96, was fond of
serving lettuce at the beginning of state dinners in order to torture his
guests, who were forbidden to fall asleep in his presence. Somewhere
along the line, lettuce became associated with opiates and was frequently
employed as an opium adulterant. Thomas Johnson listed a species he
called *"Lactuca sylvestris, major odore Opii"* or "large, wild, opium-scented
lettuce" in his *Herball* of 1633, also reporting: "saith Dioscorides, mix the
milkie juice hereof with Opium in the making thereof."

John Evelyn spoke more broadly of lettuce's herbal uses in 1699,
although noting its soporific qualities and also, bizarrely, its purported
effects on human morals, reporting that: " . . . it allays Heat, bridles
Choler, extinguishes Thirst, excites Appetite, kindly Nourishes, and,
above all, represses Vapours, conciliates Sleep, mitigates Pain, besides the
effect it has on the Morals, Temperance, and Chastity." In his *American
Medicinal Plants* of 1892, Charles F. Millspaugh, taking a more balanced
view, wrote that "although Lettuce has been considered narcotic from
ancient times, still it is but slightly soporific . . . and hardly deserves
. . . the reputation writers have made of it." However, as late as 1933, a
Mrs. Grieve reported in her *Modern Herbal:* "In the United States, after

importation from Germany via England it [lettuce milk] is said to be used as an adulterant for opium."

Oak-leaved varieties of lettuce are agreeably ancient cultivars, described in the sixteenth and seventeenth centuries in Europe, and noted by John Evelyn, among other herbalists, in his *Acetaria* of 1699. Royal Oakleaf Lettuce is a modern descendant of these ancient varieties, bred both for its elegant, more elongated "oak-leaved" form and brilliant, sunny green coloration. Certainly, there are frillier, flashier, more aggressively colored lettuces available, but not a one can touch this lovely loose-leaf for sheer refinement of tone and texture. In fact, this is such an attractive lettuce, I would almost be tempted to use it as a border plant in a purely decorative flower garden. Royal Oakleaf is also particularly notable for its uniquely sweet, almost nutty flavor, as well as for the fact that it is extremely heat tolerant and may be grown and harvested even in the swelter of mid-summer.

Lettuces are generally extremely easygoing in terms of their cultural needs, although it is reported that, in ancient Greece, Aristophanes got his best results by irrigating his lettuce beds with *oinomelite,* a mixture of honey and wine. In any case, the most important thing is to keep seedlings evenly watered, whether started indoors or out, as they can shrivel in a second if left to dry. Re-sow every 3 or 4 weeks or so for a continuous harvest through the season. Why not use these brilliantly green, elegantly cut leaves as a bed for a summery Salad Nicoise? Scatter portions of freshly seared tuna, steamed *haricots verts* and tiny potatoes, a handful of Nicoise olives, and a few anchovies over the top, then dress nicely with a tangy vinaigrette.

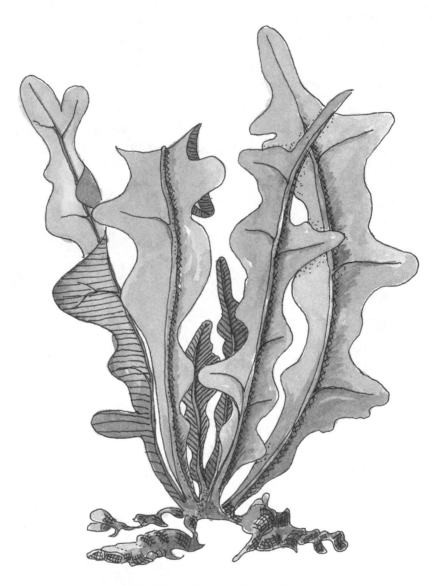

Royal Oakleaf Lettuce

RUNNER BEAN 'PAINTED LADY'

ꙮ 59. Runner Bean 'Painted Lady' ꙮ
Phaseolus coccineus

Beans have been considered so valuable a food source throughout the history of man that, among other examples, the great Aztec ruler Montezuma reportedly demanded five thousand tons of them a year in tribute from his subjects.

Green beans originally made their way to Europe by way of the Spanish conquistadores at the turn of the sixteenth century, where, culinarily, they were immediately embraced as more refined relatives of the fava and broad beans (*Vicia fabus*) that grew natively in Europe. Still, generally, they were treated as either shelly or dried beans, "shelly" signifying that they were "shelled" or removed from the pod before consumption. It is said that Phillip Miller, who ran the Chelsea Physic Garden in London, was the first person to advocate eating the young beans, pod and all, in the early eighteenth century.

The early history of the 'Painted Lady' Runner Bean is somewhat vague, but it is generally thought to be a tropical American species. Thomas Jefferson planted them at Monticello in 1812, noting: "Arbor beans white, crimson, scarlet, purple . . . ," and they may have been grown as early as the mid-seventeenth century in England. This beautiful variety of Scarlet Runner Bean is most notable for its absolutely stunning bicolored flower, boasting blazing red standards contrasted with white wings and keel. One can only suppose that this elegant cultivar takes its name from that less than subtle application of "rouge" on the feminine white cheek of the flower. It is, however, also known by the romantic and historically resonant name of "York and Lancaster."

For those of you who weren't paying attention in history class, the Yorks and the Lancasters were the opposing cousins in that long duel for the throne of England known as The War of the Roses. Heraldically, the

Yorks were represented by the white rose and the Lancasters the red and, running through that battery of Richards and Henrys made famous by Shakespeare, the Yorks and Lancasters warred through four generations. Ultimately, Henry VII, a Lancaster, claimed the crown by defeating the much maligned Yorkist Richard III at Bosworth Field. He then proceeded to marry Elizabeth, daughter of the Yorkist king Edward IV, so that, for once and for all (and "Harry and England" one presumes), Lancaster (red rose) was recommingled with York (white rose) into the Tudor line. And also, of course, into the 'Painted Lady' Runner Bean.

These beautiful and productive vines will grow to 10 or 12 feet, so do provide a stout teepee. The rough-flat, sweet, fleshy pods themselves can grow up to 10 inches long but, to be exceedingly blunt, runner beans are not the most tender in the bunch, so pick them at 6 to 8 inches long while the pod is still relatively smooth. If they reach the "hairy" stage of their maturity (it's nice to know that men aren't the only living things that suffer from this indignity), it's best to treat them as a shell bean.

In terms of sowing, plant the pretty, pinkish brown-streaked seeds 1 inch deep in well-prepared soil after the last frost, keeping in mind that beans are not fond of cool, damp weather. You should have a trellis or teepee positively laden with delicious fruit and glorious blossoms in about 65 to 70 days. Culinarily, for the more mature pods, treat the shelled beans as you would a fresh lima: boiled until tender, then tossed with some fresh-shucked corn kernels, a bit of butter, and some salt and pepper for a succulent summer succotash.

❧ 60. Runner Bean 'Sun Bright' ❧
Phaseolus coccineus

Beans were considered so invaluable in Britain in the Middle Ages as fodder for man and beast that the penalty for stealing even a handful from a field was death.

As we have mentioned previously, beans are among the oldest and most revered vegetables on earth. They have been used as food, fodder, counting and voting devices, and articles of devotion and tribute throughout the long history of man. For instance, among the early Celts, a "Beano" or bean-fest was held regularly in honor of the fairies, and in ancient British lore, ghosts and other undesirable spirits could be dispersed if one spit beans at them. I have tried this socially on several occasions with only mixed results.

Let us here, as well, deal with the historically insistent bean issue of what early *Herballs* refer to as "windinesse." It seems that flatulence was an astoundingly urgent social concern for many citizens of the fifteenth and sixteenth centuries. Sir Richard Burton mentions a total of sixty-four possible remedies for it in his *Anatomy of Melancholy* of 1621. This unfortunate aftereffect, we now understand, is due to the body's inability to metabolize some of the complex sugars found in beans. This duty is, therefore, left to the friendly bacterias of the lower intestinal tract, which, unfortunately, produce a "gaseous" effect. However, as every schoolchild knows, the more this occurs, "the better you feel," so our considered advice is still to "eat beans at every meal!"

Scarlet Runner Beans are one of the oldest varieties in existence, used ornamentally and ceremonially by the indigenous cultures of South America, transported to Europe in the fifteenth century, then back home to colonial North America in the eighteenth. It is interesting to note that many South American cultivars were forced to wend their way to Europe before they found their way to the northern end of their own

Runner Bean 'Sun Bright'

continent. These sultry climbers, called "garden smilax" by the British herbalist John Gerard and blossoming with a profusion of stunning scarlet flowers, were initially grown purely ornamentally when they reached Europe, Gerard growing them "over the arbors of banqueting places" in his own gardens in 1687.

Developed at the dawn of our newest millennium and offered by Thompson & Morgan, the Scarlet Runner 'Sun Bright' is one of the most exciting new vegetable cultivars to come along in a great while. A copiously decorative viner, Sun Bright runs quickly and brilliantly over fences and trellises, its vivid red blossoms borne in clusters like sweet peas and lasting throughout the summer, followed by large, green, stringless pods containing beautifully mottled seeds. But by far the most entrancing thing about 'Sun Bright' is the glorious and totally unique color of its foliage: a bright, startling, almost chartreuse gold. In fact, these sunny vines are so beautiful, you'll be tempted to train them up trellises in your most decorative gardens!

As with all originally tropical cultivars, runner beans need it hot to perform optimally. Therefore, plant Sun Bright seeds in moist, well-warmed up and well-drained soil and in full sun. Sow 5 or 6 seeds about 2 inches deep, placing seeds no farther than 3 inches away from the trellis or support, then thinning to the strongest 3 plants. These beans have a rich, "beany" sweet flavor when picked young but, as with all runners and some humans, can be somewhat brittle and coarse-fleshed in maturity. A wonderful bean to keep dried, use this one for a wintry potage with potatoes, onions, a handful of crushed sage, and a good meat broth.

❧ 61. Sea Kale ❧
Crambe maritima

Although Sea Kale has grown wild along the rocky seacoasts of western Europe for centuries, it actually got its name in Greco-Roman days, when it was pickled for long sea voyages and consumed as a preventative against scurvy.

Sea Kale is the true loner of the vegetable kingdom, as solitary and wild as some horticultural Heathcliff on the moors. Also known as "Sea Colewort," Sea Kale is not actually a kale, meaning a member of the *Brassica oleracea* family, at all, but is, rather, a member of the *Crambe* family, var. *maritima* (of the sea), of which the most visible member is the perennial flowering plant *Crambe cordifolia*. Also called "Heartleaf Crambe," this nonedible variety is a handsome plant for the decorative border, boasting large, heart-shaped, deep green leaves, and frothy sprays of delicate, white flowers in summer.

Sea Kale has always had its most notable popularity in Great Britain, where it has probably grown since the days of the dinosaurs, John Evelyn reporting in 1699: "Our sea-keele (the ancient crambe) . . . growing on our coast, are very delicate . . . . " However, except for those few souls still living in wild Sea Kale areas in England, this is a plant virtually unknown to consumers anywhere else. As early as 1885, the French botanist Vilmorin offered this telling observation: "Like rhubarb, the use of sea kale is at present almost confined to English people at home and abroad. It has gone to America and the antipodes, but has not crossed the Channel!"

As he reported, however, Sea Kale did manage to find its way to the New World with the first English settlers and, in 1823, Thomas Jefferson was known to have ordered some of its signature blanching pots for Monticello from a Richmond potter. Sea Kale is grown for its succulent

SEA KALE

shoots, which, similar to asparagus, arise from the roots each spring. In order to temper Sea Kale's somewhat bitter demeanor, the shoots are blanched with Sea Kale pots (or by heaping soil upon them), and, when harvested at 6 to 10 inches long in April, they are famously "asparagusy," mild, and tender.

The plants themselves are substantially handsome specimens, growing to 3 feet, with heavy, glossy green leaves, fringed and curled, and, if left to bloom, a pretty froth of white blossoms much like their *cordifolia* cousins. As the stands mature, there will be plenty of shoots for blanching (the handsome terra-cotta blanching pots adding, of course, their own fine architecture), and still enough flowering side shoots to produce a handsome display. But the crowning eccentricity of this Heathcliff of plants is that, in most parts of the world, it is one of the handful of vegetables that is perennially hardy, over which there should be riotous rejoicing.

The best way to achieve Sea Kale is to take root cuttings or buy plants propagated from root cuttings. Otherwise, sow seeds outside in spring in full sun and deeply dug soil, about an inch deep, thinning to 6 inches apart. It will most probably take a year or even two for the plants to establish themselves sufficiently to bear or even be cut for further root division, but they are well worth their tasty perennial splendor. In Great Britain, Sea Kale is often referred to as "winter asparagus" and, for culinary purposes, we may treat it as such: my advice is to steam the tender shoots for 4 or so minutes, then dress with a bit of butter whisked up in a pan with a shallot, a dash of vinegar, and a sprinkling of lemon juice.

❧ 62. Sorrel 'Silver Shield' ❧
Rumex scutatus

"By nature . . . assuages Heat, cools the Liver, strengthens the Heart,
is an Antiscorbutic, resisting Putrefaction, and imparting so grateful a
quickness to the rest, as supplies the want of Orange (or) Limon . . .
and therefore never to be excluded."

— John Evelyn, *Acetaria: A Discourse of Sallets*, 1699

A close relative to the common wild dock, which grows weed-like through the fields of Europe, garden sorrel is also a more distant relation to both rhubarb and buckwheat. Sorrel was under cultivation by the Egyptians as early as 3000 B.C., and the Greeks and Romans of the first millennium B.C. were said to snack on its astringent leaves both before and after banquets as a *digestif*. Sorrel reached France and Italy by the fourteen century, and the "Buckler" or "French" variety of garden sorrel was introduced into England sometime in the sixteenth. By the seventeenth century, the English herbalist John Evelyn noted that "the French Acetocella, with the round leaf," which was by then "growing plentifully in the north of England," was so meritorious in aspect as to make "men themselves pleasant and agreeable."

The name "sorrel" derives from the French word *surele*, which translates loosely to "sour," but this less than flattering apellation did little to dampen Europe's enthusiasm for this newly introduced herbal plant. From the fifteenth straight through to the nineteenth century, herbalists and apothecaries employed *Herba Acetosa* in a huge variety of tinctures and infusions, from oral diuretics, scurvy preventatives, and emetics, to poultices for boils, wounds, and chicken pox. The Old English proverb "Nettle in, dock out" celebrates sorrel's efficacy in taking the sting out of a thorn intrusion, and sorrel juice was also employed to bleach linens and polish silver. And, perhaps most interestingly, sorrel

Sorrel 'Silver Shield'

was traditionally called "Cuckoo Sorrow" or "Cuckoo's Meate" because it was believed that that silver-tongued vocalist soothed its throat with sorrel after singing.

Although Vilmorin-Andrieux called French or Buckler Sorrel "a plant of very peculiar appearance" in *The Vegetable Garden* of 1885, I am convinced it must have been the nearly metallic and certainly other-worldly beauty of its leaves that caused him to make such an assertion, for this is one of the prettiest bits of plant foliage you will ever see. Called "Buckler" after the small, medieval armored shield customarily worn or held on the arm, and, now, more commonly 'Silver Shield,' this beautiful plant's small, precisely shield-shaped leaves are the palest celadon green with an inkblot of true silver-white radiating through them. A patch of 4 or 6 plants will provide you with a sumptuous, foot-high explosion of silvery, artemesia-like brilliance from early spring right through till fall, and will do it perennially to boot. Aside from the artichoke, there is really no other vegetable plant that fills that crying need for silver-gray coloration quite so beautifully.

Fearing Burr listed 5 types of *Rumex,* including the Buckler variety in *The Field and Garden Vegetables of America* in 1863, commenting: "Amongst all the recent additions to our list of esculent plants, we have not one so wholesome, so easy of cultivation" as sorrel. A real garden trooper, Sorrel 'Silver Shield,' when established, is tolerant of consider-able neglect, and will survive poor soil, part shade, and even drought with equal aplomb. Rich in potassium and vitamins A and C, sorrel is also high in oxalic acid, which makes overconsumption by those suffering from gout, rheumatism, or kidney ailments unadvisable. But for the rest of us, I recommend employing these charmingly acidic leaves in a deli-cious, warming, lemony sorrel soup.

❧ 63. Squash 'Ronde de Nice' ❧
Cucurbita pepo

"The first zucchini I ever saw, I killed with a hoe."

—John Gould, *Monstrous Depravity: A Jeremiad*
& a Lamentation about Things to Eat, 1963

It is said that in late summer in certain parts of the United States, drivers are cautioned to lock their cars when leaving them to avoid returning to find them stuffed with giant zucchini. Certainly, anyone who has grown zucchini is acquainted not only with their astounding prolificacy, but also with the alarming proportions they can achieve if not sufficiently monitored. The entire *Cucurbita pepo* family, which includes zucchini as well as all other summer squash, is an admirably antique vegetable variety originally native only to the southern Americas, seed remains having been found in Central America and Mexico dating to 7000 B.C. From these exceedingly early southern origins, squash ultimately spread throughout the Americas and found its way to southern Europe with the homeward bound conquistadores, the oldest known European reference dating to 1591.

Known as "vine apples" to the Dutch and English settlers in the New World, summer squash was introduced into England in about 1700, where the vegetables became known as "vegetable marrows" for the creaminess of their flesh, which was thought to resemble the consistency of bone marrow. However, the initial favor they found was apparently brief, as, by the end of the eighteenth century, the English marrow had become known derogatorily as the "harrow marrow." The French, it seems, were an even less enthusiastic early audience, the eminent French horticulturist Olivier de Serries, who had obtained his squash seeds from Spain, referring to them as "Spain's revenge."

Bizarrely, the zucchini, America's favorite vegetable to give away to the unsuspecting or unlocked, although of 100 percent American stock, was actually refined to its current form in Italy and reintroduced into America sometime in the nineteenth century. The gargantuan, bulbous-ended thing with which we're all too familiar (by the way, the simple key to avoiding man-eating sized fruit is to harvest when young, at 5 or 6 inches) is, however, an entirely different kettle of squash from the diminutive 'Ronde de Nice' Zucchini. This lovely, little round summer squash, with its smooth, edible green skin striped with lighter green, looks like the blissful love child of a zucchini and a tennis ball. A French heirloom used for many generations in the cuisine of south and central France, Ronde de Nice is a terrific producer and a handsome plant, the copious globular fruit nestled in nicely cut leaves on stout vines growing to about 6 feet, and the flowers a clear, sunny yellow in color. The best part, however, is that you never have to worry about these zucchini getting out of hand in terms of heft and girth, which should be marvelous news to car owners.

In terms of culture, like all originally tropical beauties, squash like the soil and weather well warmed up. Start in 4-inch pots about a month before last frost, then plant out in well-fertilized hills, 3 plants to a hill, hills 4 feet apart, when soil temperatures reach 60 degrees. Thin to the strongest two plants per hill. Ronde de Nice are best harvested when anywhere from 1 to 4 inches in diameter, the golf ball-sized ones with their creamy white flesh delicious sautéed whole, the larger ones perfect for stuffing and baking. Why not try the 4-inch models, one to a customer, scooped out, filled with some good, hot Italian sausage, and baked: a marvelously zesty accompaniment to a midsummer, grilled supper?

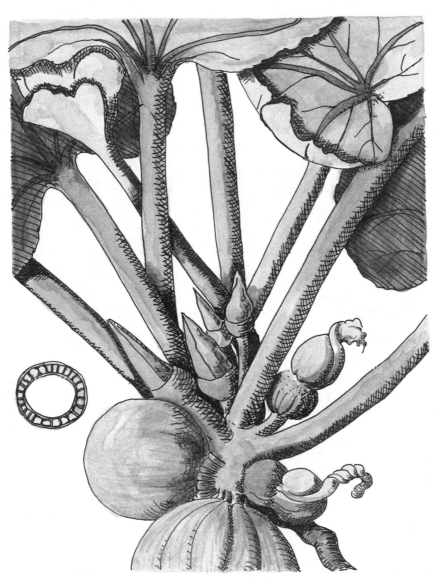

SQUASH 'RONDE DE NICE'

🎇 64. Sunburst Squash 🎇
Cucurbita pepo

*"Some of these [squash] are green, some yellow, some longish like a
gourd, others round like an apple; all of them pleasant food boyled and
buttered, and seasoned with spice."*

—John Josselyn, *New England Rarities Discovered*, 1672

Summer squash is yet another vegetable cultivar proud to be
American born and bred. Extremely ancient to South and Central
America, remains having been found dating from 7000 to 5500 B.C.
in Mexico, squash had spread from one end of the North American continent to the other by the time Christopher Columbus leapt ashore in the
West Indies in 1492. The native tribes of North America held squash in
extraordinarily high, even sacred regard, and, fortunately, were hospitable enough to pass on some of the secrets of its cultivation to our
Pilgrim forefathers. The legendary Squanto taught the first white settlers
at Jamestown how to cultivate the then totally unknown-to-them crops
of corn and squash, and, in doing so, kept them alive long enough to procreate and prosper.

In an intriguing piece of ancient Far East Indian lore, a man named
Iaia, who had used a giant squash as a casket for his dead son, desired to
look at his son one last time and, opening the squash, unleashed a torrent
of whales and other monstrous fish. Of course, this being India, the alleged
"squash" was undoubtedly that close curbit relative, the melon, which is
native to the Middle East. Be that as it may, one day four brothers who
had heard the story of the fish-laden curbit, stole it, then dropped it
when set upon by Iaia, causing it to crack open. Torrents of water and
oceanic wildlife poured forth, forming what we now know as the rivers
and the oceans of the world.

Much like the oceans, the *Cucurbita pepo* clan is somewhat daunting in its immensity, including as it does pumpkins, squash, and ornamental gourds, all of which are pretty various in their own right. In particular, squash is a *monoecious* sort, meaning it has separate male and female flowers, so bees must do the pollinating. Because bees can carry pollen from any squash to any other, there has been considerable spontaneous hybridizing over the past 3,000 years, resulting in countless varieties. The dazzling Sunburst Squash, which we recommend here, is one of the 'Bush Scallop' varieties, referred to also as "pattypans" or, in England, "custard marrows," because of their extremely fine-textured, white flesh.

As an All-American Selections Winner, the scintillating Sunburst is a presence as vibrant as the sun in the garden. These bright, daffodil-yellow colored beauties, like all bush scallops, have that wonderful flat, lobed shape that make them look almost like cartoon flowers, these particular specimens dotted with an eye of dark green at both the blossom and stem end. Additionally, Sunbursts are a bush-type squash, which means they won't sprawl, and are extremely productive, so you can expect each 3-foot bush to be positively loaded with fruit.

Sunbursts, like all squash, will respond best to good fertile soil and a lot of warmth and sunshine, do not like being disturbed, and can't abide a frost. Therefore, start seeds in 3-inch peat pots no sooner than 3 weeks prior to your last spring frost, then transplant out prior to the second set of true leaves in well-warmed soil, spacing a yard apart. As delicious as they are colorful, Sunbursts can be picked from baby size right up to 6 to 8 inches broad without losing their tender, buttery flavor. The baby ones are absolutely gorgeous for pickling.

SUNBURST SQUASH

SWEET MILLION TOMATO

65. Sweet Million Tomato
Solanum lycopersicon esculentum

The vote for "best traveled vegetable in existence" must surely go to the "Rutgers California Supreme" tomato as, in April of 1984, twelve-and-a-half million seeds of this peripatetic cultivar were sent into space aboard a satellite to circle the earth for six years, after which time they were retrieved by the crew of the space shuttle Columbia, *brought back to earth, and distributed to 3 million school children and 64,000 teachers worldwide.*

O f the five botanical families of our cultivated tomato, *lypersicon esculentum cerasiforme* is regarded as being the direct descendant of the wild tomatoes that sprang spontaneously from the Central American earth thousands of years ago. They were originally sprawly, straggly things with small, currant- to cherry-sized fruit in shades of yellow and red, although only the red type was thought to be edible. Domesticated by the Aztecs, Mayans, and Incas, they were in wide cultivation when the first conquistadores arrived, although the *Solanum lypersicon esculentum cerasiforme* still grows in a wild state throughout most of the Southern Americas.

Both yellow and red varieties of the "cherry" were brought back to Europe by the homeward-bound Spanish and Portuguese at the dawn of the sixteenth century, and they were under culinary cultivation in Italy by 1550, and in England, decoratively, by 1590. There, as we've seen, due to their shared relationship with the nightshade clan, tomatoes, along with eggplants and mandrakes, were all lumped together into one big, highly suspect mess of plant matter, believed to induce everything from rampant lust to insanity, and known assortedly and collectively as "love," "madde," or "rage" apples.

The winsome Sweet Million is certainly a descendant of one of those earliest red *cerasiforme*. A recent offspring of the twentieth-century hybrid Sweet 100, Sweet Million not only offers the same wonderfully early maturation and flavor as its popular parent, but also much better disease and crack resistance. Sweet Millions are truly the candy of vegetables: these medium-sized cherries, growing to about an inch around, are a glossy deep red in color with a burstingly sweet tang. However, it's the sheer multiplicity of the fruit that will astound you as these vigorous, indeterminate vines are literally covered with clusters of ruby-red fruit, a well-tended and supported plant capable of producing 500 or more.

One of the latest topics of conversation swirling around tomatoes is the benefit of lycopene, a major carotenoid similar to beta-carotene, currently touted as a potent antioxidant. Lycopene is also what gives tomatoes their red color: the darker the red, the higher the lycopene content, which makes Sweet Millions a healthy bunch of berries indeed. Interestingly, the tiny, deep-red fruits of the *Lycopersicon pimpinellifolium,* or South American wild "currant" tomato, contain over forty times more lycopene than our domesticated varieties. Small, however, is not necessarily best, as domesticated red Beefsteaks are also exceptionally high in lycopene.

Kudos go all around to Sweet Million for yielding early and abundantly and being so cooperatively impervious to disease and cracking. Transplant 6-week-old seedlings out 2 weeks after your last frost date and you should be picking "millions" of these sweet things 60 days from transplant. A shot of fish emulsion once halfway through the season will be welcomed as the fruit has such excellent storage characteristics, you could be eating tomatoes from the same plant for 4 months or more. These I would just wash and toss, still wet, with a sprinkle of salt and finely chopped cilantro as the world's most perfect summer snack.

ॐ 66. Tiger Tom Tomato ⚜
Solanum lycopersicon esculentum

During the years of the "Great Tomato Pill War," between 1837 and
1850, a correspondent for the Whig and Aegis *offered the observation*
that tomato pills "have one grand specific . . . a vast concentrating
power capable of drawing both fools and coppers around them."

Bizarrely, following centuries of malignment and culinary dismissal, the tomato, in the late 1830s in America, experienced a most remarkable turn of fortune and reputation as a patent medicine ingredient. Historically, thought to induce both carnality and insanity, the tomato was virtually shunned in polite society until well into the nineteenth century, as in 1728 when the Cambridge University professor Richard Bradley advised planting this highly suspect cultivar away from human habitation, "for the leaves and stalks, when rubbed by the clothes in people's passing by, yield a very strong and very offensive smell." But in 1837, the year John Miles began marketing Dr. Miles Compound Extract of Tomato, the popular tide of the lowly tomato turned.

This purportedly wildly efficacious extract was recommended for everything from constipation to affectations of the liver to scrofula and dyspepsia, the manufacturer touting Dr. Miles Extract as "one of the most valuable articles ever offered for public trial or inspection." In fact, it met with such astounding success that, in 1838, a rival, Dr. Phelps Compound Tomato Pills, Blood Purifier and Universal Panacea, hit the marketplace, publicized by the *Boston Morning Post* as "purifying the animal fluids, opening and cleansing the channels of circulation . . . and giving strength and vigor to the nerves of organic life." Whatever they may be.

Thus began the years of "The Great Tomato Pill War," a whirlwind of escalating, cross-country lawsuits, scurrilous allegations, and newspaper

TIGER TOM TOMATO

attacks and counterattacks. Other pills plunged in, Hallock's Tomato Panacea, for instance, promising "a certain remedy for . . . dyspepsia, scrofula . . . rheumatism and nervous afflictions, worms, constipation, pulmonary and bilious complaints, eruptic diseases of the skin, and all diseases arising from impure blood." In the end, however, the mutual mud-slinging served only to sink the entire tomato pill industry and, by the middle of the nineteenth century, both war and mania were over.

The wonderful Tiger Tom Tomato, a late nineteenth-century heirloom, played no part in this trans-American drama, but is surely worthy of a moment of fame in its own right. This large, beautiful, tiger-striped "cherry" is one of the many varieties saved from extinction by the legendary seedsman Ben Quisenberry of Syracuse, Ohio, who saved heirloom seeds and operated "Big Tomato Gardens" from 1910 until shortly before his death at the age of ninety-nine in 1986. In 1980, when he was ninety-three, during a stay in the hospital, Ben tragically lost twenty-two of the thirty-one tomato varieties he was propagating, including the beautiful Tiger Tom. Luckily, this gorgeous cultivar with its distinctive jagged golden stripings on a rich orange-red field was rediscovered by Kent Whealy of Seed Savers Exchange and is available to us again today.

Start Tiger Tom indoors 4 weeks before last frost and plant out 2 weeks after, when soil is well warmed up, in your sunniest location. Tiger Tom, like all tomatoes, loves compost, old manure, a pH of about 6.5, and a good, deep watering. Also, do provide some stout trellising for these vigorous, indeterminate vines to clamber up. Pretty, 2- to 3-inch round Tiger Toms have a delightfully tart taste, so how about trying these in a Tuscan bread salad by coarsely chopping six or so, then tossing with chunks of day-old Italian bread, chopped garlic and parsley, and healthy lashings of extra virgin olive oil and balsamic vinegar?

67. Trifetti Pepper

Capsicum annuum

*"A peculiar effect of capsicum is worth mentioning. In Mexico the peo-
ple are very fond of it; and their bodies get thoroughly saturated with it,
and if one of them happens to die on the prairie, the vultures will not
touch the body on account of its being so impregnated."*

—Jethro Kloss, *Back to Eden*, 1939

There are about twenty-three species of chile peppers (genus *Capsicum*), but nearly all of the cultivated varieties belong to just two: *Capsicum frutescens* (including the *Capsicum chinense* group) and *Capsicum annuum*. The *Capsicum frutescens* family includes some of the hottest peppers on earth (Habañero, Scotch Bonnet, and Tabasco among others), as well as some milder cultivars. *Capsicum annuum* contains more than 1,000 named cultivars, all sweet bell peppers and most chiles among them, including the Jalapeño, Poblano, Ancho, Bird Pepper, Cherry Pepper, Thai Pepper, Anaheim, Serrano, Paprika, Cayenne, and the object of this chapter's affection, the vivacious Trifetti Pepper.

Jethro Kloss, in his *Back to Eden*, also reported that the chile pepper was: " . . . effective as a poultice for rheumatism, inflammation, pleurisy. . . . For sores and wounds it makes a good poultice . . . . Good for kidneys, spleen, and pancreas. Wonderful for lockjaw. Will heal a sore, ulcerated stomach.. . . " In Coahuila, Mexico, the cure for the "evil eye" in children still calls for the child to be wiped with the inside of an Ancho Chile, followed by some signing of the cross. In a grand example of parallel, global usage, the people of Trinidad believe adolescent "evil eye" can be cured by wrapping seven Chiles with salt, garlic, and onion skins, then passing the pungent package seven times around the demon seed in question. On perhaps a sounder scientific note, a single chile has been found to contain not only a day's supply of beta-carotene, but nearly twice the recommended dose of vitamin C.

If I had to choose one chile to grow, it would certainly be the Trifetti. I do not hesitate to say it is one of the most spectacularly lovely plants I know. Imagine a sturdy, bushy thing with the most mesmerizing tricolored, variegated foliage, each leaf picked out in a vibrant green contrasted with both cream-colored splotches and deep purple veining in infinite variety. The dream continues to unravel itself as the dainty fruit, prolifically produced, start a gorgeous, glossy aubergine, then ripen over the season to an extremely gregarious lipstick red. So gorgeous is this extravagant creature, I use it multiply to create a 2-foot-tall hedge around my vegetable island beds and it is truly a glory to behold.

Marvelously, this striking edging also serves to deter wandering pests, who find the bite of a pepper can be a more than notable opponent. Or, if a hedge of peppers isn't in your garden plan, why not pop a few into the red section of your decorative border and watch them contribute welcome contrast while pulling their "red" weight very becomingly as the fruit ripens?

As with all peppers, start under glass 6 weeks before last frost in 4-inch pots, then plant out a foot apart when the soil has heated up to 60 degrees. Recipe-wise, why not use some of these pretties to make a pepper spray for your plants and vegetables? Just mash a few up in some water with just a splash of dish detergent (this aids in leaf adherence), funnel it into a spray bottle, and have at your favorites. From mite to mongoose (and even unwelcome guest), you'll be amazed at whom it will end up keeping away.

TRIFETTI PEPPER

☙ 68. True Lemon Cucumber ❧
Cucumis sativus

According to the ancient botanist Pliny, the Roman emperor Tiberius was so inordinately fond of cucumbers, consuming more than ten a day, that he had them grown in mobile barrows, which could be wheeled continually to the most auspicious growing climes in the empire so that he might never go without them.

Cucumbers are among the most ancient of vegetable varieties, having been thought to have originated in northern Africa, then traveling, as was the case with many early vegetables, along the silk and spice trade routes north and west into Hindustan and Asia. The excavation of the famous Spirit Cave along the Myanmar/Thailand border in 1970 yielded a trove of cucumber seeds carbon-dated to an extraordinary 9750 B.C. Certainly cucumbers were well known in Egypt as early as the monumental Twelfth Dynasty, and they were among the vegetables the Jews lamented leaving behind when they were expelled.

This was potentially an early lapse in culinary judgment considering that the Egyptians enjoyed making a popular beverage by cutting a hole in the end of a ripe cucumber, stirring the insides with a stick, closing up the hole, then burying the cucumber in a pit for several days, after which, according to John Gerard, "the pulp [would] be found converted into an agreeable liquid." One assumes this was also the moment when the famous advertising slogan "Have a cuke and a smile" was born.

If you imagine that all cucumbers are of the "long . . . green . . . rough, and set with certain bumps and risings" variety extolled by John Gerard in his *Herball* of 1636, or that all are possessed of that paranormal waxiness of skin found far too frequently in today's markets, you have clearly not made the acquaintance of the True Lemon Cucumber. This beauteous and bonified All-American heirloom was first introduced by

Samuel Wilson right here in the great U.S. of A. amidst the tranquil Quaker farmlands of Mechanicsville, Pennsylvania, in 1894.

The True Lemon, also known by the entrancing name "Crystal Apple" in the Orient, is not long or curved but round, and is usually about 2 to 3 inches in diameter when ripe. Its skin, far from being suspiciously indigestible, is ultrathin, eminently edible, and of the loveliest ivory deepening to yellow striation. In fact, one could almost mistake it for its namesake. Its fruit are borne on pretty, rambling vines studded with the deep yellow, star-shaped flowers unique to the curbit family, and they will happily clamber up a trellis or teepee with a little early direction.

As with all cucumbers, start these indoors 4 to 6 weeks before your frost date, then set out, with an absolute minimum of root disruption, only when soil temperatures are above 65 degrees and night temperatures won't dip below 60 degrees. A floating row cover will dissuade most of the early pests and provide some shelter from the noonday sun for early transplants. You should be sampling your first pretty lemon in 60 to 70 days. These sunny, thin-skinned beauties are so surprisingly mild, digestible and sweet, there's no need to peel or seed. I recommend cubing them, then tossing with yogurt, fresh pepper, chopped mint, and a squeeze of lemon. The result is a coolly refreshing West Indian *raita:* the perfect accompaniment to a piquant chicken or lamb dish.

TRUE LEMON CUCUMBER

TURKISH ORANGE EGGPLANT

🎄 69. Turkish Orange Eggplant 🎄
Solanum integrifolium

"A Turk won't marry a woman unless she can cook eggplant at least a hundred ways."

— Iris Love, the *New York Times,* February 4, 1971.

Although generally India seems to be the home site of choice for the original cultivated eggplant, some feel it is Arabia that deserves this particular plaudit, citing mentions of the eggplant in the works of Avicenna in the fourth century A.D. The common name "aubergine" comes to us via the Sanskrit *vatin-ganah,* which literally translates as "anti-flatulence vegetable," signaling perhaps the most highly debated of all early medical conditions, "winde," its panoply of cures having been topics of infinite variety and amusement for countless early societies. *Vatin-ganah* later became *badin-gan* in Persian, then *al-badindjan* in Arabic, *alberginia* in Catalan, and finally the familiar *aubergine* in French. The English adopted "aubergine" in the late eighteenth century, leaving the less worldly "eggplant" to serve as the preferred common name of the rustic infidels and outcasts of Australia and America.

Turkey has long been a country well known for the depth and breadth of its eggplant-based cuisine. In fact, as early as the fourteenth century A.D., the Turks were legendary for a dish called *Imam Bayaldi* or "fainting priest," some lore holding that this personality-filled moniker derives from the tale of a Muslim holy man so overcome by the heavenly aroma of the dish that he fell into a swoon. Others hold that the real derivation of this tale lies in an old Turkish proverb: *Imam evinden ash, olu gozunden yash cikmaz,* which translates to "No food is likely to come out of a priest's house and no tears from a corpse." This tale purports that, far from being transported to the land of the insensate on the frigate of deliciousness, the parsimonious priest was, in fact, shocked into a faint by the too extravagant use of olive oil in the dish.

The Turkish Orange Eggplant (*Solanum integrifolium*), an ancient Turkish heirloom, is one of the most visually distinctive members of this highly decorative family. The small, one might even say "bite-sized" fruit is, when fully mature, a brilliant deep orange as rich and glossy as Chinese lacquer. Prior to full maturation, the fruits, which begin green, turn a delightful light orange with pretty green stripings and are borne on vigorous bushes, each of which will produce twenty fruits or more during the growing season. In fact, these plants are considered so ornamental by many plantsmen, they are often seen container-grown for their sheer decorativeness.

Sow seeds indoors 8 to 10 weeks before the last frost in 5-inch pots. Harden off slowly as eggplants are very sensitive to transplant shock. Eggplants should be picked when the skin is taut and glossy and, in this case, still showing some green. When cut open, the seeds embedded in the flesh should be nearly invisible: the color of the flesh itself. The bite-sized fruit of the Turkish Orange Eggplant make it, simply halved, a superb choice for *caponatas* and curries, but I suggest you try a classic Turkish eggplant salad of a summer's eve. Roast a dozen or so unpeeled in the oven until charred on the outside, then cool and peel. Squeeze as much water as possible out of the soft pulp, then mash with a sprinkle of lemon juice, a generous pinch of salt, a clove of garlic, and a drizzle each of olive oil and vinegar. Serve festively garnished with sliced tomato and Turkish olives. Try not to faint.

70. Watermelon 'Moon & Stars'
Citrullus lanatus

Ancient Roman legend maintains that, when a watermelon was thrown at the Roman governor Demosthenes during a political debate, he promptly placed it upon his head and thanked the donor for the gift of a helmet to sport during his upcoming war with the Macedonians.

It was none other than the great missionary-explorer David Livingston who settled, for once and for all, the question of the origins of the watermelon when, while journeying through the Kalahari Desert of Africa, he came upon endless acres of watermelons growing wild. However, as the ancient words for watermelon in such diverse languages as Arabic, Berber, Sanskrit, Spanish, and Sardinian seem to be unrelated, culture in all those countries is of immense antiquity. The first watermelon harvest on record was depicted in an Egyptian tomb painting dating to the third millennium B.C., and watermelons were often placed in burial tombs to provide sustenance in the afterlife.

Watermelons were then spread along the Mediterranean by way of silk-road traders and, by the tenth century, had found their way to China, now the world's biggest producer. By the thirteenth century, watermelons were common throughout Europe, although the word *watermelon* didn't appear in an English dictionary until 1615. Watermelons were brought to the Americas by the earliest Spanish and Portuguese colonists, commonly cultivated as far north as Massachusetts by 1629, and mentioned by Father Marquette, French explorer of the Mississippi, in the Midwest by 1673.

Watermelons are approximately ninety percent water and even today, districts in Africa cultivate watermelons for that purpose alone. That said, watermelons also have zero fat or cholesterol and loads of vitamins A and C, and are importantly high in both fiber and potassium, making them, for all their aqueous content, a health food indeed. Over 1,200

WATERMELON 'MOON & STARS'

varieties of watermelon are currently grown worldwide, over 4 billion pounds produced per annum in the United States alone. According to *The Guinness Book of World Records,* Bill Carson, of Arrington, Tennessee, holds the record for the largest watermelon known to man, his proud offspring weighing in at a gargantuan 262 pounds.

The legendary cultivar 'Moon & Stars' is an indisputable dazzler: a lovely, oval, dark-to-almost-black green fruit covered with brilliant yellow "stars" and, usually, one larger, luminous, cadmium dot designated as the "moon," and looking for all the world like a garden-grown, celestial globe. Equally dramatic is its deep, beautifully cut, green foliage, as beautifully spotted with daffodil yellow as the fruit. The early history of this imposing melon is somewhat obscure, although the great American seedsman Peter Henderson of New Jersey introduced it in 1926, and by 1935, both Henry Fields of Iowa and the Robinson Seed Company of Nebraska were offering it as well. Then, for some reason, 'Moon & Stars' went into a dark, nearly extinct period until, thankfully, in 1981, it was rediscovered on a farm near Macon, Missouri, by Seed Saver's Kent Whealy. As is so often the case, all vegetable gardeners are in his debt.

'Moon & Stars,' like all watermelons, requires a good, well-warmed soil, a well-fertilized sand or sandy loam being the best. Therefore, start indoors and plant out 10 feet apart in all directions after danger of frost has passed. Raised beds are also to be recommended because they allow for the excellent drainage to which melons are partial. You should be harvesting these striking melons in about 80 to 95 days. Enjoy their sweet, pink flesh in a cool, summery salad: seeded, cubed, and tossed with a confetti of cucumbers, fresh peas, and a tangy citrus vinaigrette.

🎗 71. West Indian Burr Gherkin 🎗
Cucumis angurra

*The irrepressible eighteenth-century English diarist and biographer
Dr. Samuel Johnson said of the cucumber: "A cucumber should be well
sliced and dressed with pepper and vinegar, then thrown out as good
for nothing."*

L et's put it this way: the cucumber, in comparison to other vegetables, is not a big, raucous bundle of vitamins, minerals, and
beneficial substances. The average cucumber is, in fact, 96 percent
water. Food historian Waverly Root said that the cucumber is "as close
to neutrality as a vegetable can get without ceasing to exist." And,
although Charlemagne declared the cucumber his favorite fruit, eating
them in custard tarts, they are, as with all vegetables of some history and
interest, steeped in culinary controversy.

The *Apocrypha*, those biblical works of equally controversial authen-
ticity, sermonizes that "a scarecrow in a garden of cucumbers keeps
nothing." Not a very uplifting appraisal. Seventeenth-century English
medical authorities cautioned that cucumbers filled the body with "cold
noughtie humors." Sleeping on a bed of cucumbers, however uncom-
fortable, was said to cure a fever: thus, "cool as a cucumber." In any case,
cucumbers of various varieties have been around forever, have their
uses, aesthetic and otherwise, and none more so than this one.

The West Indian Burr Gherkin is a descendent of the African *Cucumis
longipes* and was introduced into Jamaica from Angola in the seventeenth
century via the Portuguese slave trade. It has commonly been called the
West Indian Gherkin, due to the mistaken belief, dating to the eighteenth
century, that the West Indies was its place of origin. Also known as
Jerusalem Cucumber, Prickly Fruited Gherkin, Wild Cucumber, Maroon
Cucumber and (erroneously) Gooseberry Gourd, it was introduced into
the United States by Minton Collins of Richmond, Virginia, in 1793.

This is a wonderfully odd-looking fruit: a short, plump oval thing about 2 or 3 inches long, covered as densely as a porcupine in prickly, pale green spines. The gherkin plant itself is a vigorous trailing vine, 5 to 10 feet long, with hairy, ridged stems bearing, at each node, a 1- or 2-inch tendril along with 2 to 4 very pretty, pale yellow flowers, a leaf petiole, and the occasional fruiting branch. The small, deeply cut, five-lobed leaves are very attractive and similar to those of the watermelon. To see this lovely green and yellow architecture clambering up a teepee or trellis, festooned with pendant, spiny burr gherkins is really a marvelous, even slightly zany sight in the garden.

Cucumbers prefer a rich soil and don't plant them out until the soil temperature has reached at least 70 degrees (few vegetables are as intolerant of cold soils). If you wish to begin them early, use a floating row cover kept tightly sealed until the plants are about 6 inches tall. Also, feel free to interplant or companion plant with corn, squash, or other cucumbers, as this variety will not cross-pollinate. Consistent moisture throughout their season, which is 65 to 70 days, will help prevent bitterness.

The greenish flesh of the West Indian Burr Gherkin is unlike that of other cucumbers in taste and texture, being somewhat prone to bitterness, so pick them when under 1½ inches long for optimum taste. The past-picking fruit is verifiably bitter and seedy, but makes a wonderful visual addition to a late-summer or fall centerpiece piled up in a bowl with some squash and miniature pumpkins. Culinarily, why not try the young fruit in your favorite pickle recipe, as they're awfully pretty in a big jar or glass pickle barrel?

WEST INDIAN BURR GHERKIN

72. Windsor Broad Bean
Vicia faba major

*"And it came to pass, when David was come to Mahanaim, that Shobi . . .
and Machi . . . brought wheat and parched corn, and beans . . . for the people that were with him to eat. For they said: the people are hungry and
weary and thirsty in the wilderness."*

— Samuel II:17, 27–29

The Broad or Faba (Fava) bean, also called Field, Winter, Tick,
or Horse Bean, vies with the carrot, pea, and cucumber for
being, potentially, the oldest single vegetable known to man. A
hoard of 2,600 well-preserved broad bean seeds, dated to 6500 B.C., was
excavated from a Stone Age settlement near Nazareth in northern Israel,
and numerous remains of *Vicia faba* have been discovered in archaeolog-
ical excavations in the Mediterranean basin and central Europe dating to
the third millennium B.C. In short, it is an ancient vegetable variety legendary for its seeming invincibility to frost and heat, excellence fresh or
dried, and fitness for both human and animal.

However, by the first century A.D., as palates became more demanding with the increased cultivation and refinement of edible plants, the
patricians of Rome and Greece peremptorily banished broad beans from
their plates, judging them a vulgar, coarse-podded, nearly indigestible
item fit only for cattle or the poor. The ancients of Rome and Greece,
however, did continue to use the seeds in their voting and elections:
white seeds signifying a "yes" vote, black signifying "no," thus the term
"black-balled," rightfully "black-seeded." Plutarch's dictum, "abstain
from beans," far from being an anti-flatulent warning, actually signifies
"stay out of politics."

The Windsor Broad Bean (*faba* var. *major*), a refined and cultivated
descendant of those early, previously shunned types, is richly deserving of

its nominative kinship to the British royal family as it is an exceedingly regal plant. Broad beans are remarkably different in appearance from "green" (*Phaseolus vulgaris*) beans because, for one thing, their pretty ovalate and lanceolate, grayish-green leaves look more like those of a pea than a bean. As well, their highly scented flowers are also typically pealike: white with black-purple blotches. But it's the bean pods themselves, which form symmetrically at near right angles along the entire length of the elegant 2- to 3-foot stems that are their chief architectural attraction. A patch or row of these is a wonderfully handsome thing in the garden.

Windsor Broad Beans are also a wonderful choice for more northerly climes because, unlike other beans, they can be planted in cool soil and weather. If planted early, harvest can begin as early as July, about 14 to 18 weeks after sowing, and last until frost. Harvest the pods when small (3 inches long) for cooking whole, or pick for shelling when the bean shape appears in the pod walls. You will discover the oval- or kidney-shaped beans inside are quite large and flat. If, when you open a pod, the little "scar" on the bean is darker than a pale, greeny white, the beans have reached an advanced state of maturity and will definitely need to be shelled for cooking.

Fresh bean seeds need only be boiled for 10 to 15 minutes, but broad bean seeds that are stored dried are cooked for about an hour and a half after soaking them in water overnight. During this last phase, you might as well toss in some chicken stock, a hambone, some diced celery, carrot, and onion, and a good handful of salt, pepper, crushed sage, and thyme for an excellent winter potage. Oddly, broad beans are violently toxic to certain people of Mediterranean origin, so please pay close attention to your roots before ingesting.

☙

WINDSOR BROAD BEAN

WOOD'S PROLIFIC BUSH SCALLOP SQUASH

❧ 73. Wood's Prolific Bush Scallop Squash ❧
Cucurbita pepo

So immense were some of the first "askutasquash" viewed by the early and perhaps overly morally engrossed Pilgrims that they considered them "uncivilized to contemplate."

Our word *squash* comes to us from the Algonquin Indians of Massachusetts, and is a derivative of the word *askutasquash,* meaning "eaten raw or green." Although squash originated in the southern Americas, they could be found growing nearly wild from one sea to the other in the north by 2000 B.C. in a numbing variety of shapes and sizes and colorations, as squash crossbreed zealously. A mystic plant in Native American lore, the squash was the equivalent of the "primal egg" of Hindu mythology, one charming tale telling of the Maize Goddess who had two suitors: the Bean and the Squash. When she agreed to marry the Bean, he was so enthralled that he remained glued to her side, winding her tightly in his embrace. The bereaved Squash, however, ran off all over the ground to hide his sorrow, which is why Beans climbed the cornstalks in a Native American garden, while the Squash meandered dejectedly between the rows.

Native Americans also believed that squash, like other native vegetables, held important medicinal powers, so they chewed squash seeds to treat worms and consumed massive quantities of the plant's flesh to treat snakebite. The early colonists drank liquefied squash for bladder trouble and munched squash for a variety of ailments, ranging from the pains of childbirth to toothache and cold. The early settlers of Jamestown, Virginia, recommended boiled squash mashed into a paste as a poultice for sore eyes, and in 1611, in an early bid for American beauty, a Miss Elizabeth Skinner of Roanoke, Virginia, advocated an application of squash seeds mixed with cornmeal to remove freckles and other unsightly "spottes" from the face.

The White Bush Scallop, an ancient variety also sometimes known as Pattypan or even Peter Pan, was additionally called "Symne" in 1648, and "Cymling" by Thomas Jefferson in 1803. "Cymling" is still the most common name for it in the South. It was illustrated by the French botanist Matthias Lobel as early as 1591, and was certainly known throughout Europe by the early seventeenth century. Wood's Prolific Bush Scallop, bred for its tidy bush habit, was first offered by T.W. Woods & Sons of Richmond, Virginia, in 1899.

The fruits are truly lovely things, almost resembling blossoms with their rounded, flattened spherical shapes and pretty fluted edges. Their colors can range from a creamy white to a luna-moth-like pale, pale green, and the fruits are borne in great profusion on handsome plants that refuse to sprawl, lavish with the marvelous, almost prehistoric-looking leaves common to squash and the additional dash of appealing yellow blossoms. These pale beauties will produce right up until frost if harvested continuously and are best picked while young, before the rind has thickened.

Seedlings may be started 4 to 5 weeks prior to the last frost provided that the roots are minimally disturbed during planting, peat pots being particularly useful for this purpose. Alternatively, seed may be sown after the danger of frost is past, when the soil temperature reaches a minimum of 65 degrees. Sow 2 inches deep, 3 to a hill, in hills spaced about 3 feet apart. Thin to the strongest 2 plants. I make these into a delicious, curry-scented summer soup by cubing and simmering with leeks and potato in chicken broth, liquefying, then adding a bit of cream, a good dose of curry, and a healthy pinch each of salt and pepper. Chill and serve studded with nasturtium blossoms. Lovely.

❧ 74. Yellowstone Carrot ❧
Daucus carota sativus

In 1974, Englishman Basil Brown, who could only be described as a health nut, consumed ten gallons of carrot juice and took 10,000 times the recommended dose of vitamin A, turning his skin a bright, jaundice yellow and resulting in severe liver damage and his untimely death ten days later.

Carrots found favor with our most ancient civilizations very early on, seeds having been unearthed from the tombs of the pharaohs dating to the third millennium B.C. By 702 B.C., they were also being grown by Merodach-Baladan, Chaldean king of Babylon, who cultivated them with the scented herbs in his garden, suggesting that they were used for their fragrant flowers and foliage alone. The exact lineage of the cultivated carrot has always been difficult to trace as it was not always distinguished from the ancient parsnip, the name *Pastinace,* from the Latin verb *pastinare,* "to dig up," being employed for both. Confusion seemed to reign until the eighteenth century, when the Swedish botanist Carl Linnaeus finally gave the carrot and parsnip their current, discreet classifications, *Daucus carota,* and *Pasticaca sativus,* respectively.

The early Arab writer Ibn al-Awam gives a twelfth-century description of two varieties of carrot growing in the Mediterranean basin: a red one, which he described as tasty and juicy, and a yellow-and-green one, which he lamentably found "coarse and inferior." During the sixteenth century, the avid Dutch began their cultivation and refinement of the carrot, the historically popular purple variety falling out of favor and the yellow carrot stepping up into the spotlight. Carrot juice was also employed by the famously resourceful and economy-minded Dutch to enhance the appearance of their paler cheeses, and carrots are still used in France to brighten the color of butter. Additionally, the Dutch were

YELLOWSTONE CARROT

fond of feeding carrots to their prized holstein cows, which ultimately gained for them the reputation of being the producers of the richest, most vibrantly yellow butter in Europe.

The Yellowstone Carrot is a modern hybrid descendant of those earlier yellow types, and is being recommended here because of its real, true, buttery yellow color and long, straight, broad-shouldered growing habit, which readily identifies it as one of the noble Imperatore types, the whole topped with the feathery mop of handsome green foliage. As well, unlike a good many other paler-fleshed carrots, Yellowstone is notable for its sweet, crisp taste and smooth-fleshed texture. Being a brawny, long-limbed sort, Yellowstone requires a sandy, well-drained, and deeply tilled soil to grow optimally. Broadcast seed thinly in a row or patch in early spring, covering the seed thinly as well, and water gently. Thin to 2-inch spacing in all directions, and these sumptuous, sweet, golden roots should be ready for harvest in about 85 days.

In deference to this vegetable's venerable history, I provide a carrot recipe from Apicius Czclius (A.D. 14–37), who was the author of the "Apician" cookbook, reputed to be the oldest known to man. Apicius is also remembered as a demanding lunatic of a gourmand, fond of feasting on flamingo brains, parrot heads, and vegetables sprinkled with gemstones of an evening; however, his *De Re Coquinaria* is still thought to encapsulate the best of the art of Roman cooking, as well as provide a provocative glimpse into the lifestyle of the Roman aristocracy before the fall of the empire. Among other carrot recipes, Apicius advises serving them raw and grated, with a simple sprinkling of salt, olive oil, and vinegar, a recipe that still delivers a wonderfully and sinfully fresh, sweet tang.

❧ 75. Zebra Hybrid Eggplant ❧
Solanum melongena

"I wish Englishmen to content themselves with meats and sauce of our own country than with fruit eaten with apparent peril; for doubtless these Raging Apples have a mischevious qualite, the use whereof is utterly to be forsaken."

— John Gerard, *The Herball*, 1687

Eggplants, as has been discussed, are one of those extravagantly maligned vegetables that had to wage a considerable uphill battle towards culinary acceptance. Reputedly originating in India, they are first recorded as being cultivated in China as long ago as 500 B.C., although it is entirely possible they were originally grown purely decoratively, as was their cousin the tomato. We know the small, white, egg-shaped variety was perhaps the earliest incarnation of this vegetable, but the Chinese had certainly developed their signature long, thin, purple-tinged varieties by the second century A.D., and the pioneering German physician and botanist Leonhart Fuchs reports on both yellow and purple cultivars in that country as early as 1543.

The Arabs, who had been growing eggplants since at least the fourth century A.D., introduced eggplants to Europe in the Middle Ages in that familiar silk/spice road scenario of import and trade typical to cultivars originating in the Far East. However, the eggplant did not really permeate greater Europe until the sixteenth century and even then had to twiddle its thumbs around the Mediterranean basin until people managed to surmount the various nightshade-related suspicions attached it. As late as 1586, Rembert Doedoens, the Dutch herbalist, claimed they induced "evil humors" and called the eggplant "unwholesome," as if it could and would influence children's tender psyches adversely if consumed.

By 1885, Vilmorin-Andrieux listed fifteen varieties, one, the "Striped" or "Guadeloupe" Eggplant, described as having a "peculiar variegation . . . striped, lengthways, with pale purple on a whiter ground." Fearing Burr also listed this same variety in America in the nineteenth century. There are several descendants of these original, striped eggplant I could recommend to you, including the evocatively named Italian heirloom varieties 'Rosa Bianca' and 'Listada di Ganda,' but here I will commend to you a contemporary cultivar: the Zebra Hybrid Eggplant.

To my mind, for sheer, epicurean beauty, there is no other eggplant or, really, any vegetable, to surpass it. The fruits, growing to a handsome 6 to 8 inches long and 4 inches wide as they slowly emerge from their elegant gray-green blossom casings, assume a truly voluptuous stature and are striated in the most beautifully unique shades of deep, rich, rusty violet and white. As well, the Zebra Hybrid is prized for its mild, creamy flesh with absolutely no trace of bitterness: all in all, perfect attributes in either mate or vegetable.

As with all eggplants, the Zebra Hybrid will be passionate about heat, so they'll need to be started in the greenhouse or your sunniest window 6 weeks before your last frost date and planted out only when soil and nighttime temperatures are well above 60 degrees. Eggplant's principal pest is the flea beetle, which attacks the young seedlings, so be on guard with some kind of covering at this early stage unless you want leaves pin-pricked into skeletalness. With such voluptuous fruit, the plants will also benefit greatly from a stout stake and some attention to keeping them tied up. Pick these gorgeous fruits, on the small side, when about 5 to 6 inches long and still shiny (usually about 70 days from transplant). Due to their extravagantly uniform shape, Zebra Hybrids are perfect for slicing into thick rounds, brushing with rosemary-scented oil, and throwing onto a hot, late-summer grill.

Zebra Hybrid Eggplant

❦ Resources ❦

I have availed myself of infinite sources in my quest for the fascinating intricacies of vegetable history, lore, and culture, and wish to thank all those listed below as well as the many more, especially the ones searched and found over the Internet that I may have neglected or forgotten. In particular, I wish to thank the seed houses I rely on, who are saving our vegetable heritage as they enrich it with new cultivars, and who inspired me to write this book in the first place.

SEED SOURCES

Baker Creek Heirloom Seeds
  2278 Baker Creek Road
  Mansfield, MO 65704
  (417) 924-8917
  www.rareseeds.com

The Cook's Garden
  PO Box 1889
  Southampton, PA 18966
  (800) 457-9703
  www.cooksgarden.com

Nichols Garden Nursery
  1190 Old Salem Road NE
  Albany, OR 97321
  (541) 928-9280
  www.nicholsgardennursery.com

Park Seed Company
  1 Parkton Ave
  Greenwood, SC 29647
  (800) 213-0076
  www.parkseed.com

Pinetree Garden Seeds
  PO Box 300
  New Gloucester, ME 04260
  (207) 926-3400
  www.pinetree@superseeds.com

Redwood City Seed Company
  PO Box 361
  Redwood City, CA 94064
  (650) 325-7333
  www.batnet.com/rwc-seed

John Scheepers Kitchen Garden Seeds
  23 Tulip Drive
  PO Box 638
  Bantam, CT 06750
  (860) 567-6086
  www.kitchengardenseeds.com

Seeds of Change
  PO Box 15700
  Santa Fe, NM 87592
  (888) 762-7333
  www.seedsofchange.com

Seed Savers Exchange
  3094 North Winn Road
  Decorah, IA 52101
  (563) 382-5990
  www.seedsavers.org

Southern Exposure Seed Exchange
  PO Box 460
  Mineral, VA 23117
  (540) 894-9480
  www.southernexposure.com

Territorial Seed Company
  PO Box 158
  Cottage Grove, OR 97424
  (541) 942-9547
  www.territorialseed.com

The Thomas Jefferson Center for Historic Plants
Monticello
PO Box 318
Charlottesville, VA 22902
(434) 984-9822
www.twinleaf.org

Totally Tomatoes
334 West Stroud Street
Randolph, WI 53956-1274
(800) 345-5977
www.totallytomato.com

Underwood Gardens
1414 Zimmerman Rd.
Woodstock, IL 60098
(815) 338-6279
www.underwoodgardens.com

Vermont Bean Seed Company
334 West Stroud St.
Randolph, WI 53956
(800) 349-1071
www.vermontbean.com

BOOKS

Acetaria: A Discourse of Sallets
Evelyn, John
Brooklyn Botanic Garden
1937

Blue Corn & Square Tomatoes:
Unusual Facts About Common Garden Vegetables
Rupp, Rebecca
Garden Way Publishing
1987

The Brooklyn Botanic Garden Gardener's Desk Reference
Marinelli, Jane
Henry Holt & Co.
1998

Burpee: The Complete Vegetable & Herb Gardener
Cutler, Karan Davis
Macmillan
1997

Cornucopia: The Lore of Fruits & Vegetables
Roberts, Annie Lise
Knickerbocker Press
1998

Culpeper's Complete Herbal
Culpeper, Nicholas
Kessinger Publishing Company
2003

Field and Garden Vegetables of America
Burr, Fielding
The American Botanist
1988

Garden Sass: The Story of Vegetables
McDonald, Lucille
Thomas Nelson, Inc.
1971

Gerard's Herbal
Gerard, John
Spring Books
1964

Green Immigrants: The Plants That Transformed America
Haughton, Claire Shaver
Harcourt, Brace, Jovanovich
1978

Herbs, Salads and Tomatoes
Shewell-Cooper, W.E.
John Gifford, Ltd.
1972

The Origins of Fruit & Vegetables
  Roberts, Jonathan
  Universe Publishing
  2001

Rooted in America: Foodlore of Popular Fruits and Vegetables
  Wilson, David Scofield & Angus Kress Gillespie
  The University of Tennessee Press
  2000

The Tomato in America: Early History, Culture, and Cookery
  Smith, Andrew E.
  University of Illinois Press
  2001

The Vegetable Book: An Unnatural History
  Lovelock, Yann
  St. Martin's Press
  1972

The Vegetable Garden
  Vilmorin-Andrieux, M.M.
  John Murray, Ltd
  1885

Vegetables from Amaranth to Zucchini
  Schneider, Elizabeth
  William Morrow
  2001

WEBSITES

www.Botanical.com

www.HungryMonster.com

www.KillerPlants.com

www.DavesGarden.com

www.HerbalMagic.com